THE SUIT

D1286697

The Suit

Form, Function and Style

CHRISTOPHER BREWARD

REAKTION BOOKS

For James

Published by Reaktion Books Ltd
Unit 32, Waterside
44–48 Wharf Road
London N1 7UX, UK
www.reaktionbooks.co.uk

First published 2016, reprinted 2016, 2021
Paperback edition first published 2021
Copyright © Christopher Breward 2016

Printed and bound in India by Replika Press Pvt. Ltd

A catalogue record for this book is available from the British Library

ISBN (hb) 978 1 78023 523 3
ISBN (pb) 978 1 78914 496 3

Contents

Three-piece pinstriped double-breasted wool suit made in 1937 by Radford & Jones, UK, for the British patron and collector of Surrealism Edward James.

INTRODUCTION:
The Tailor's Art

The gentleman's suit is one of those overlooked but enduring symbols of modern civilization. For almost four hundred years it has been held up by artists, philosophers and critics as evidence of humanity's unceasing and transformative search for perfection. Through its fitness for purpose, its sleek elegance and its social grace it has become a perfect example of evolutionary theory and democratic utopianism made material. The Viennese architect Adolf Loos, father of modernism and occasional fashion journalist, was one of those suitophiles for whom fine tailoring signified holiness. He wrote an influential series of short articles in the years around 1900 that positioned the bespoke and everyday objects of the contemporary gentleman's wardrobe as archetypes of progressive design. Hats, shoes, underwear and accessories were scrutinized for the qualities that set them in competition with the inferior output of more 'vulgar' industrial sectors (women's dress) and nations (Germany). For Loos the suit was a fundamental component of an enlightened existence, a signifier of civilization older in origination even than Laugier's hut, that prehistoric model for the classical temple.[1] The suit had seemingly always been there to remind man of the responsibilities and prizes attached to his higher state:

> I have only praise for my clothes. They actually are the
> earliest human outfit. The materials are the same as the

> cloak that Wodin, the mythical Norse leader of the
> 'wild hunt'[,] wore . . . It is mankind's primeval dress
> . . . [It] can, regardless of the era and the area of the
> globe, cover the nakedness of the pauper without adding
> a foreign note to the time or the landscape . . . It has
> always been with us . . . It is the dress of those rich in
> spirit. It is the dress of the self-reliant. It is the attire
> of people whose individuality is so strong they cannot
> bring themselves to express it with the aid of garish
> colours, plumes or elaborate modes of dress. Woe to
> the painter expressing his individuality with a satin
> frock, for the artist in him has resigned in despair.[2]

The earnest consideration of clothing by literary and artistic Vienna a century ago operated in an intellectual context far removed from the more superficial concerns of much early twenty-first-century celebrity- and brand-focused public fashion discourse. The social, economic and spatial circumstances in which clothes are made, sold, promoted and worn have also developed in myriad ways. But the suit itself, as worn and understood by Loos, survives in barely modified form as an item of everyday and formal wear in most regions of the world. Its apparent demise as a relevant component of work, leisured and ceremonial dress has been trumpeted by successive pundits, although its unobtrusive yet ubiquitous contours still furnish the bodies of men and women in all walks of life, from politicians to estate agents, bankers to rabbis, courtroom defendants to wedding grooms.

This book, in its tracing of the suit's all-pervasive influence in modern and contemporary cultures, will attempt to do justice to Adolf Loos's faith in his clothes; to show how the suit's simple solutions have emerged and how its original meanings persist and adapt to denote truths that are greater than a basic meeting of cloth, scissors and thread. In order to do so, it will

Adolf Loos, father of architectural modernism and champion of the bespoke suit, 1904.

be necessary to start with the fundamentals, with the form of the suit itself.

Bespoke (fitted to the customer's precise measurements and handmade locally by master craftsmen) or ready-to-wear (pre-sized and mass-manufactured across a network of often distant factories by hand and machine), the suit as we know it now conforms to a basic two- or three-piece structure, generally made in finely woven wool or wool mix with a canvas, horsehair and cotton (or synthetic cotton) interlining to provide structure, and a silk or viscose lining. Its fabrics have always been an integral element of the suit's appeal and an important marker of its quality. The selection of smooth worsteds, soft Saxonies and rough Cheviots, divided into standard baratheas, military Bedford cords, glossy broadcloths, sporting cavalry twills, work-aday corduroys, elegant flannels, strong serges, hardy tweeds and homespuns, and dressy velvets, dictates the colour, texture, fit, handle and longevity of a suit, and is often the first consideration in the process of specification. The choice of weave and design – plain or Panama, hopsack or Celtic, diagonal, Mayo, Campbell or Russian twill, Bannockburn or pepper and salt, pinhead, birdseye, Eton stripe, barleycorn, herringbone, dogtooth, Glenurquhart or Prince of Wales check, pin- or chalk-stripe – becomes the key to a customer's character.[3]

In made-up form, the suit is usually characterized by a long-sleeved, buttoned jacket with lapels and pockets, a sleeveless waistcoat or vest worn underneath the jacket (if three-piece) and long trousers. The simplicity of its appearance is belied by the complexity of its construction, as a recent comparative study of ready-made suit manufacture commissioned by the British Government Department of Trade and Industry demonstrated:

> A tailored jacket has an intricate structure, composed of as many as 40–50 components . . . Its manufacture may involve up to 75 separate operations. The first step

A selection of tweeds, Anderson & Sheppard, Savile Row, London, 2010.

in the production process is the 'marker' – a pattern
according to which the many components . . . are cut
from the material . . . The production sequence is, in
principle, similar to making cars. The various parts are
made first, they are then assembled into sub-assemblies,
which are progressively brought together for final
assembly. Smaller items are made . . . in parallel with
the body fronts – interlinings, back sections, pockets,
collars, sleeves, and sleeve linings. Pockets and
interlinings are attached to the body front. Back
sections are joined to the fronts, then collars. Sleeves
are lined and then joined to the body. Buttonholes and
buttons are added . . . A range of mechanical presses,
each with a moulded shape, are used for top pressing
the completed garment.[4]

The analogy with the automated production-line processes
of car manufacturing is, however, misleading. As the authors
of the report go on to explain, the almost sensile, embodied
nature of the product entails an attention to the idiosyncracies
of the individual suit style, impossible to achieve through total
mechanization:

The favoured approach is the 'progressive bundle'
system, whereby all the parts needed to make a suit
are bundled together, and are progressively assembled.
Operators are grouped according to the section of the
garment on which they work and the work is passed
between them. The system has the flexibility to cope
with variations between one suit and another, with
training and absenteeism.[5]

The contemporary ready-made suit, then, is the product of a
widely recognized and well-ordered system of manufacture,

refined and democratized throughout the twentieth century by high-street pioneers and international brands, and present in the wardrobes of many. Its bespoke variation continues to be manufactured on traditional lines, for an elite minority in the West and a wider audience in Asia and the developing world. Both options conform to an accepted set of parameters that produce a fairly standardized and familiar necessity, almost boring in the predictability of its form. But it was not always thus. When the proposition of a 'suit' of clothing (a well-fitted set of garments to be worn at the same time, although not necessarily of matching cloth) emerged in Europe's cities and royal courts during the fourteenth century, its construction was more likely to constitute a complex negotiation between the skill of the tailor and other craftsmen and women, and the tastes and desires of the client. The possibilities for variation were endless.

Surviving letters of the sixteenth and early seventeenth centuries between members of the nobility and their agents who were procuring dress items for them in London and elsewhere, and early autobiographical accounts of sartorial choices, betray an intense consideration of several variables regarding price, quality of materials, detail of cut and construction, colour and adherence to notions of fashionableness, modesty and courtly style, all complicated by the more specialized circumstances of the clothing trades in this period. The commission of one 'suit' of clothes would involve transactions with several tradesmen, from the cloth merchant to the tailor, the button- and buttonhole-makers, the embroiderer and so on.[6]

The tailor's role in all this shifted radically towards the end of the sixteenth century, as competing trades jostled for primacy in the hierarchy of Europe's powerful guild system (dominated as it was by wealthy, influential wool and silk interests). In Florence and Venice during the 1570s and '80s his role in creating the fashionable look of the final outfit was sometimes still seen as negligible. One Venetian trade guide suggested that

Making clothing is nothing more than draping cloth over a person and cutting away the excess and that is how the garment is made. Afterwards anyone can add decoration and therefore tailors always learn from their customers and carry out whatever task they ask for and nothing more.[7]

Anderson & Sheppard, a traditional Savile Row tailor, 2010.

But the situation changed as tailors achieved greater professional independence and commercial clout, earning the right to select and acquire cloth and other materials direct from fellow merchants, rather than receiving them, along with instructions for achieving the final look, from the client. Increasing skills in cutting, forming and embellishing cloth also resulted in the production of workshop sketchbooks, recording and demonstrating the diverse solutions available for the construction and finishing of a sleeve or a cloak, and in a growing number of widely circulated printed tailors' pattern books and international costume guides. By the beginning of the seventeenth century it was becoming clear that the heightened entrepreneurial and creative prowess of the tailor was positioning him such that he could dictate, rather than follow, the vagaries of fashion.[8]

Alongside this interpretation of growing professional confidence among the suit's producers, one should perhaps also consider the influence of a shifting idea of the nature of fashion among critics and consumers of male dress over the same period. Academic histories of men's clothing have often drawn connections between politics and appearances. In 1930 the psychologist John Carl Flügel described a 'great masculine renunciation' of ostentatious 'peacock' fashion among late eighteenth-century men of taste, brought about by the rise of industrialization and democracy. Serious times called for sober dressing. More recently, the social historian David Kuchta has identified a much earlier simplification of the male wardrobe in the French and English courts of the mid-seventeenth century.[9] This, he suggests, was less a reflection of the growing influence of the sober values of a rising mercantile and industrial class than a consequence of political, philosophical and religious debates about the responsibilities of aristocrats and monarchs that had begun in the 1630s and '40s. Flügel had suggested that

> As commercial and industrial ideals conquered class
> after class, until they finally became accepted even by
> the aristocracies of all the more progressive countries,
> the plain and uniform costume associated with such
> ideals has, more and more, ousted the gorgeous and
> varied garments associated with the older order.[10]

Dudley North, 3rd Baron North, a principal courtier at the court of James VI and I of Scotland and England, resplendent in a black suit embroidered in silver thread. Unknown artist, *c.* 1615, oil on canvas.

Kuchta makes counterclaims for the replacement of what he has termed the 'old sartorial regime' (in which the costly 'mingle mangle' of gorgeous aristocratic apparel, condemned in the 1580s and '90s by puritan pamphleteers as immoral and unpatriotic, but insisted upon by the authors of princely conduct books as a duty to magnificence and conspicuous consumption by the honour of a ruling order bound to maintain the visible hierarchical structures of luxury production and consumption) with a redefined, post-Restoration construct of responsible governance, clothed, quite literally, in the suit: the uniform of modern manners.[11]

Whether one takes the chronology and emphasis of Flügel or of Kuchta as a guide, the concept of 'renunciation' is in many ways an attractive and compelling idea, essentially binding sartorial developments to the emerging political values of modern democracies. But as an argument for the genesis of a particular style of dressing, it is perhaps too Anglocentric. England was not the only country to introduce a revolution in masculine dressing. The simple ideal of the suit also arose at various moments in Scandinavia, the Low Countries and other parts of Europe. Its sombre uniform was taken up as eagerly by the merchants of the seventeenth-century Dutch Republic as by officers of the Directoire in France or provincial professionals in Biedermeier Austria. In its focus on political theory, the renunciation idea also fails to respect the power and presence of the tailored object itself, or the skill and clout of its makers. Reformed aristocrats and newly emancipated capitalists may well have adopted the suit as an appropriate badge, but the origin of its meanings and the nature of its material forms lie much closer to the circumstances of its physical production than to its political symbolism.

Regardless of the debates concerning renunciation, the design principles and philosophical ideals that had attended the evolution of the suit's material form as a repository of

Habit de Tailleur

Nicolas de Larmessin II, *Costumes Grotesques; Habit de Tailleur (tailor)*,
1695, etching and engraving with hand colouring on laid paper.

The Tailor's Workshop by the Dutch artist Quirijn Gerritsz. van Brekelenkam, 1661, oil on panel. A client consults the tailor while workers adopt the traditional sewing posture, cross-legged on a bench.

contemporary values throughout the eighteenth century persisted into the nineteenth. Concepts of measurement and standardization continued to affect the suit's evolution, both as an object and as a symbol. They informed the Victorian transition from bespoke to more sophisticated ready-made suit manufacturing for a widening range of customers by the late nineteenth century. The introduction of the tape measure and an interest among tailors in standardized measuring and cutting techniques from the 1820s both eased the possibility of mass-production techniques and offered a promise of democratization to an industry that at its higher, more dandified and also scientific end was already fascinated by the reforming potential of Platonic notions of the model 'classical' body.[12]

Tailors in Renaissance Florence and Regency London would have recorded or translated clients' physical proportions as notches on individualized lengths of paper, whose marks came together to construct a unique cloth carapace. By the early years of Victoria's reign the provision of published guides presenting mathematical systems of proportion as universal tailor's laws lent the trade the ability to fit and adapt a generalized pattern to anyone who desired it. The transformative effects of padding, lining and darting ensured a fit that could almost compete with the work of the best West End master of bespoke craftsmanship, at least from a distance.

Furthermore, as standardized templates replaced archives of personal measurements in all but the most elite businesses, the possibilities of controlling the forms and speeding up the outcomes of seasonal fashion changes on both the national and international stages multiplied significantly. Shifting templates for the idealized fashionable body could now be imposed simultaneously on a massive scale, where formerly the fashionable look was built up on a more individualized, almost ad hoc manner, according to local desires. In a sense, the new, rationalized tailoring systems were providing maps for the navigation of an unexplored corporeal terrain, which in the context of empire and an expanding masculine commodity culture was becoming subtly eroticized.[13]

Edward Giles, the editor of the London-based tailor's trade journal *The West End Gazette*, produced a history of such systems in 1887, illustrating their impact and assessing their usefulness. Many of them were published to service a greatly expanded and newly professionalized industry. *Mr Golding's Tailor's Assistant* of 1818 is just one early example; it proposed that all measurements be taken from the notion of a perfectly proportioned male figure 'whose breast measure exceeds the waist about an inch, and whose waist length exceeds the breast width an inch'.[14] Giles noted that the search for 'grace and elegance' based on abstracted ideal proportions, typified by Golding's approach, merely produced temporal approximations of beauty that accorded with the prevailing sartorial taste. This meant that the forms soon became outmoded:

> The hollow curved lapels, the skimpiness of the waist,
> the amplitude of the skirts, the extreme fullness of the
> top of the sleeves . . . combine to make a man appear
> to us as a figure of fun.[15]

Later systems abandoned a striving for the ideal in favour of the scientific rigour of anatomical study and geometry. Such an approach seemed better fitted to remedying the actual imperfections of living bodies through skilful adaptations of scale and proportion. Rather than attempting to impose a perfected model on all physical variations, systems published from the middle of the nineteenth century recognized the reality of differing body types and promoted a degree of flexibility. *The Complete Guide to Practical Cutting* of 1847 acknowledged that men's bodies could not be reduced to the angle of a set-square and a series of algorithms. Its authors 'found by experience that a corpulent man's coat, when cut by proportions of his breast measure, produced a coat too large behind and consequently too small in front'.[16]

Such arcane tailoring debates went to the heart of contemporary questions of mechanization and its effects. Charles Compaing and Louis Devere, in their *Tailor's Guide* in the 1850s, offered for the consideration of cutters a comprehensive survey of body shapes and postures that gave priority to human judgement rather than industrial precision. Their rhetoric is as rich in metaphor as any produced by Thomas Carlyle, Karl Marx or William Morris:

> Inventors have neglected the fact that no machine
> can give a correct measure of a flexible substance like
> the human body, because a piece of wood, leather
> or metal cannot feel as the hand does, whether the
> pressure or stretching is hard enough, which is an
> essential thing in measuring . . . It would be ridiculous
> to call on a customer and wrap him in a machine. Any
> man, whatever his build, can always be measured with
> the greatest accuracy by means of the common inch-
> tape . . . Customers seem not to have patience enough
> . . . They do not like to be measured, and looked at in
> every way . . . and they are vexed that their tailor sees
> they are not the very type of the Apollo Belvedere.[17]

Herein lay a profound disconnection between the everyday reality of the tailor's trade, to which close proximity to and understanding of the client's individuated body was fundamental, and a world in which new technology and concepts of scientific progress were seemingly smoothing out inefficiency and irregularity. George Atkinson, who claimed to have pioneered the use of a standardized tape measure as early as 1799, asserted in a self-promotional pamphlet of the 1840s that he

Lapel construction, Anderson & Sheppard, 2010.

had 'reduced the trade of the tailor to a system'. It was a system in which the suit was starting to take on the qualities and associations of a refined industrial product, although Atkinson continued to value the human touch: 'I found that by constantly using [the measure] I could judge the size of a gentleman by my eye.'[18]

Judgement, skill and taste were the attributes raised most forcefully in the publications of the most famous nineteenth-century tailoring reformer, the German mathematician Dr Henry Wampen. His first work, *The Mathematical Art of Cutting Garments According to the Different Formations of Men's Bodies* (1834), was followed in the 1850s by *Anatomy and Anthropometry*, and in 1863 by *Mathematic Instruction in Constructing Models for Draping the Human Figure*. Wampen adopted a highly technical approach. His self-consciously academic prose was engineered as an improving aid for raising the standards of the tailoring profession, and as encouragement to those setting up tailoring schools. As he stated, 'culture of the mind is the first element wherefrom arises all that civilizes and improves us and by which means all men become equalized.'[19]

Besides elevating the status and aspirations of the suit-maker, Wampen suggested that the consideration of Platonic ideals of beauty and the appreciation of the naked male form in its perfect 'classical' state might also have some role to play in the design and manufacture of contemporary men's clothing. Recalling his early career, he noted:

I went as a student to Berlin to complete my studies. I took a great interest in art and philosophy, and a question was then much discussed whether the Grecian ideal of beauty was simply ideal or founded upon scientific basis . . . I was induced to measure certain statues, and I came to the conclusion that the Grecian sculptors worked on a scientific basis . . . One day a tailor who worked for me, a Mr Freitag, saw my sketches on a table when he said 'You are just the man we want; you must write something for us tailors.'[20]

Such claims about anthropometry and classicism, and the theoretician's understanding that the physiques depicted in ancient Greek sculpture should form an exemplary template for the production of a rationalized modern wardrobe, were all well and good, and clearly precede the interests of modernists such as Loos in the man's suit as universal Platonic form. But it is most unlikely that the complex equations of writers in the elite tailoring journals meant much to the jobbing high-street tailor. In the expanding business of mass-produced men's clothing such airy philosophizing must have been irrelevant at best. Yet in a broader sense the circulation of such ideas mirrored popular concerns about the display of the male body and its fitting-out in appropriate clothing, thereby contributing much to the material evolution of the suit as we understand it today.

These concerns were especially palpable at that delicate moment when an abstract pattern was transformed into a second skin for the customer. The alchemical role of the tailor in translating paper, chalk, tacking thread, pins and cloth into a suit of clothes fitted to the frame of the customer represented a magical form of skill, but one that has generally remained invisible. The very private processes of measuring and fitting have been overshadowed by those moments in the workshop or the street that have been prioritized by historians of labour and by literary and cultural historians, concerned as they have been with tracing histories of the sweated industries or the highly public footsteps of the dandy. The crucial ritual of measuring the client may have slipped from view because of its intensely personal nature. Here was a problematic physical proximity the social implications of which did not escape the attention

John Finch, 1st Baron Finch, Attorney General and Speaker of the House of Commons, adopting the simpler wardrobe and sober linen (despite the ceremonial gold embroidery) of the mid-seventeenth century. After Van Dyck, *c.* 1640, oil on canvas.

Henry William Pickersgill, *Captain Thomas Drummond*, 1834,
oil on canvas. Here the civil engineer and founder of modern surveying
adopts the black uniform of the rising professional classes.

of trade journalists, music-hall performers and even popular novelists. Even as recently as the 1990s, the over-familiar tailor was a stock character in British television comedy, originator of the ubiquitous catchphrase 'Suits you, sir!'[21]

These awkward one-to-one negotiations involving limbs and torsos took on added significance in the 1880s and '90s, as the provision of more sophisticated ready-to-wear garments in new outfitters' shops and department stores started to compete with the traditional domain of the bespoke tailor. The columns of *The Tailor and Cutter*, a leading British trade journal, were often concerned with the strict protocol surrounding the application of tailoring systems to living bodies. The aptly named correspondent T. H. Holding urged readers:

> Remember that your hands are going about a sensitive intelligent man and not a horseblock. First rule – never stand whilst taking any measures in front of your man, but on his right side. To do so is to commit a gross piece of familiarity, rather offensive in all cases . . . The leg measure is one of the very chief measures in a pair of trousers, and is often taken very faultily. With great quickness place the end of your measure close up into the crutch, then pass down your left behind his thigh . . . If a man's dress is right, well two measures thus 24, 22, will at once indicate which side has to be cut out.[22]

Old-fashioned etiquette, therefore, in combination with the modernizing rhetoric of sizing systems and pattern-cutting techniques, characterized the new language of tailoring and informed the social meanings and appearance of the suit in Europe and America at the turn of the twentieth century. It also coincided with a considerable transition in terms of style. The remit of the average man's wardrobe expanded to include a greater number of standardized garments associated with leisure pursuits, particularly sport, whose influence could not help but inform the look and feel of the tailored suit. The lounge suit, for example, whose softer surfaces and comfortable, simplified cut had previously been reserved for domestic relaxation, was accepted for business wear on both sides of the Atlantic by about 1910.[23] Its sleeker form and lighter weight were a natural complement to the healthy, modern male physique.

Similarly, in bespoke tailoring trends in the 1890s, design techniques strove to produce a finished article that promoted a sense of modernity and flattered the body within. Interestingly, debates in the trade on whether the best method for achieving this was through padding and lining or through rational cutting methods have continued to the present. These different styles of tailoring are often associated with national models (for example, relaxed and 'unstructured' Italian tailoring) or company traits (the formal, military styles associated with various Savile Row firms). In 1898 the editor of *The London Tailor* paid close attention to the differences:

> The new style is what we have termed the 'cast iron pattern of tailoring' . . . We made . . . for a customer a very soft Vicuna coat without stiffening or padding, nothing more, in fact, than French canvas and a bit of the thinnest horsehair in the shoulder. The coat was nice to the touch . . . and . . . fitted him like a glove. He goes 200 miles away for a sojourn in a health resort and gets a [new] coat . . . From the front part . . . back to the shoulder seam . . . had been strained out until the pattern in the checked tweed was enlarged almost double the width . . . The shoulders were like epaulettes . . . The one [style] was neat and natural and the other unnatural and absurd. But then from Portsmouth to Aberdeen it is the style . . . Nothing we

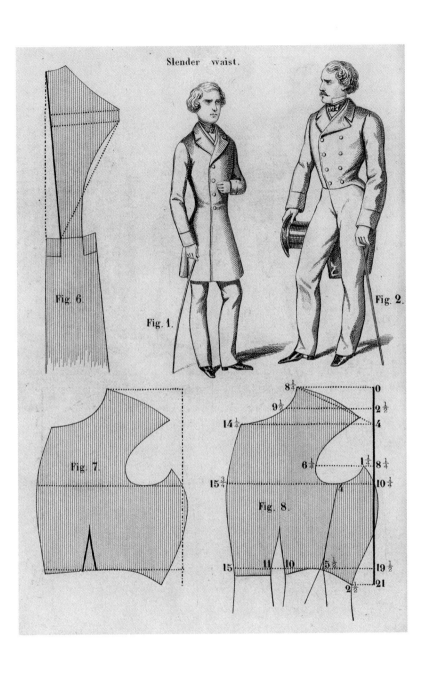

Slender waist.

Fig. 6.

Fig. 1.

Fig. 2.

Fig. 7.

Fig. 8.

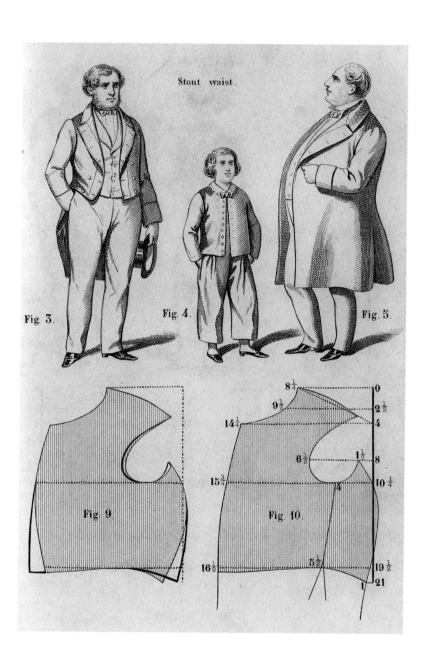

The Tailor's Guide: A Complete System of Cutting Every Kind of Garment (c. 1850). Manuals like these promised that the anthropometric craft of the suit could enhance all body shapes.

can say is ever going to bring us back to that natural free-like tailoring that is to us so artistic . . . It is much easier to put a piece of cloth on a man's breast, and stiffen it out as though . . . with thin tin, than to get a coat right that shall sit in its place.[24]

It is extraordinary that such debates have continued to hold currency into the first decades of the twenty-first century. The industrial report of 2003 quoted above posed a number of questions to a hypothetical British suit manufacturer set, against the odds, on commercial success. These rehearsed arguments about fit, embodiment, style, skill, efficiency and consumer understanding that would have been familiar to our Florentine tailor of the 1580s, and certainly to our West End master in the 1890s:

The producer would have to ask himself whether he has the designers who understand how to construct a better suit – one which feels and looks good because it has the three-dimensionality to adapt itself to the human body, 'breathes' and is pleasant to handle? Could he find technicians who understand how to translate that design into a sequence of manageable cutting and sewing operations? Could he train and retain the employees capable of carrying out these more intricate operations, accurately and to time? Is he prepared to invest in the necessary equipment . . .? And is he able to communicate the refinements of a better suit to a market that does not understand many [of] the subtleties of such a suit, either by developing a powerful brand name, or by selling to exclusive retailers?[25]

The long-lived arguments over the material, philosophical, aesthetic and political qualities of the suit frame this book, as

Costume—1911—Men

English
national Gazette 1911

A Tailor's Fashion Plate, c. 1910. By the early twentieth century the lounge
suit was the costume synonymous with business.

The spectacular Galeries Lafayette, opened in Paris in 1912, was one
of many department stores whose novel approaches to distribution and
retailing aided the democratization of the suit and shifted the emphasis
from bespoke to ready-made production.

By the mid-twentieth century ready-made suits were ubiquitous, and a staple of high-street trade.

well. We will consider in detail the suit's functional and symbolic meanings, and its association with particular social groups and forms of labour. We will trace the suit's status as a vessel for trade and nationalist sentiment, and its varied development in different parts of the world. We will investigate the suit's adaptability as an icon both of mainstream fashion and of oppositional style; and we will consider its currency in a wider sense, as inspiration for artists and writers in mainstream culture and of the avant-garde. The suit is a complex, enduring vessel of meaning whose form raises questions about identity that continue to challenge us today. When the art historian Anne Hollander wrote her own influential reflection on the cultural importance of the suit in modernity in 1994, she too expressed a simultaneous sense of frustration and fascination at its confounding, enduring and self-contradictory power, which still resonates. Her opening observations on the successor to Wodin's cloak offer an appropriate segue into the following discussions:

> Although male heads of state wear suits at summit
> meetings, male job applicants wear them to interviews,
> and men accused of . . . murder wear them in court . . .
> the pants-jacket-shirt and tie costume, formal or informal,
> is often called boring or worse. Like other excellent and
> simple things we cannot do without, men's suits have
> lately acquired an irksome aesthetic flavor, I would say
> an irritating perfection. Their integrated subtle beauty
> is often an affront to post-modern sensibilities, to eyes
> and minds attuned to the jagged and turbulent climate
> of the late twentieth century. Current millennial impulses
> tend towards disintegration, in style as in politics; but men's
> suits are neither post-modern nor minimalist, multi-cultural
> nor confessional – they are relentlessly modern, in the best
> classic sense. They seem moreover to be surviving.[26]

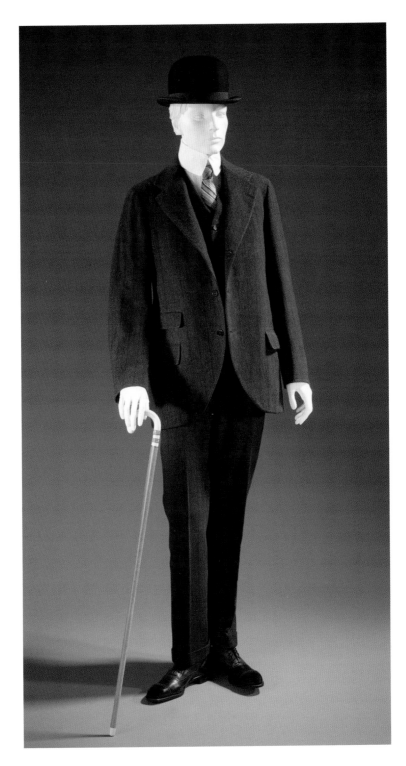

Man's lounge suit, wool twill, 1911.

DUKE OF NORFOLK.

Henry Howard, 6th Duke of Norfolk, in a version of the transitional
Ottoman vest style associated with Charles II's reform of English Court
dress in 1666. Gilbert Soest, *c.* 1670–75, oil on canvas.

ONE

Well Suited

Although the skill of the tailor and the pressures of commercial culture have produced a material and stylistic history of the modern suit that is marked by subtle variation and an obsession with detail, many observers and critics have instead chosen to damn it for its association with a stifling conformity. The suit has most often been dismissed as a mere uniform, regulating difference by disciplining appearances – keeping men in their place. Edward Carpenter, the progressive late nineteenth-century writer on social struggle and sexual freedom, railed characteristically against the prison of its heavy seams and drapes:

> The truth is that one might almost as well be in
> one's coffin as in the stiff layers upon layers of
> buckram-like clothing commonly worn nowadays.
> No genial influence from air or sky can pierce this
> dead hide . . . Eleven layers between him and God!
> No wonder the Arabian has the advantage over
> us. Who could be inspired under all this weight
> of tailordom?[1]

Carpenter's lament is an interesting one, not least in its evocation of the comparative freedoms of Arabian dress. For if we take Charles II's introduction of the Ottoman-inspired vest into English Court dress in the autumn of 1666 as the pivotal moment in the birth of the modern three-piece English suit, then we can see, as John Evelyn, Andrew Marvell and other contemporaries did, that Orientalism was in fact one of several influences that inspired the look of the first suits (hardly the marker of a stifling conformity).[2] The new costume adopted by Charles's courtiers also achieved an unprecedented and welcomed uniformity among elite and middling civilian ranks, which in its earliest iterations was revolutionary and invigorating rather than constraining. Samuel Pepys recorded the effects with typical acuity:

> This day [15 October 1666] the King begins to put
> on his vest, and I did see several persons of the House
> of Lords, and Commons too, great courtiers, who
> are in it – being a long cassock close to the body, of
> black cloth and pinked with white silk under it, and
> a coat over it, and the legs ruffled with black ribbon
> like a pigeon's leg – and upon the whole, I wish the
> King may keep it, for it is a very fine and handsome
> garment.[3]

Fine and handsome it may have been, but the new suit also owed a debt to the military uniforms that had preceded it, and which were being reformed at the same time. In response to the increasing use of firearms on the battlefields of Europe in the sixteenth and early seventeenth centuries (particularly around the time of the Thirty Years War, 1618–48), military theorists and commanders had come to the conclusion that greater coordination and cooperation of troops (within and between, for example, musketeers using gunpowder and pikemen with their steel) were necessary in order to gain martial advantage. A concurrent gradual shift from the use of private feudal armies, mercenaries and conscripted civilians towards the establishment of permanent salaried regiments of volunteers was also a pre-condition for the manufacture, provisioning and development of uniform military dress across all ranks (aided by the possibilities for standardization and mass production introduced by the tailoring systems we noted in the Introduction). By the beginning of the eighteenth century, in what has become known as the 'patrimonial era', a striking and polychromatic uniformity of battle-zone and ceremonial dress, often informed and embellished by aspects of local or imported costume (from plumes to leopard skins), had become the norm.[4]

In Bourbon France, with its spectacular fetish for hierarchical and bureaucratic order, the military uniform was a potent agent of court and state control – and thus a source of much debate. This continued through the French Revolution and into the Napoleonic Wars. The material and economic costs and rewards generated by the uniform business were huge. Daniel Roche, a historian of clothing and appearances, estimates that in the middle of the eighteenth century (between about 1726 and 1760), in order to clothe the necessary number of recruits to keep regiments fully manned, the French army's suppliers had to provide 20,000 outfits a year. For foot soldiers alone this would have accounted for a theoretical 30,000 metres of broadcloth for coats; 3,000 metres of coloured cloth for facings; 100,000 metres of serge for linings; and further thousands of metres of various textiles for breeches, waistcoats, shirts, underwear, stockings and neck stocks.[5] But what was more important than the scale of the project, in France and elsewhere, was the disciplinary challenge that the idea of uniform set down, both for civil society in general and for concepts of respectable, fashionable and modern masculinity in particular. As Roche proclaims, drawing on the philosophy of the time:

> The need to shape minds and bodies finds in uniform
> a valuable aid: it is a training, an element in the
> education of controlled individual power . . . It is
> an instrument in a process designed to shape the

Captain George Kein Hayward Coussmaker resplendent in the uniform
of the First Regiment of Foot Guards. Military uniform was the main driver
for fashion change in European and North American male clothing from
the mid-eighteenth century. Joshua Reynolds, 1782, oil on canvas.

physique and the bearing of a combative individual,
whose autonomy conditions his docility and whose
obedience transforms individual strength into
collective power. Uniform is at the heart of the
military logic . . . when war is a necessary continuation
of politics. Uniform constructs the fighting man
for mortal combat. It imposes control, a source
of efficiency in battle and means to social power . . .
It creates through education, realizes a personage
and affirms a political project by demonstrating
omnipotence . . . Uniform is central to a utopian
and voluntarist vision of the social which reconciles
the conflict between automatic docility 'and the
concrete economy of the individual liberty in which
the autonomy of each constitutes the measure of his
obedience'. It impregnates the whole of society.[6]

Roche's oblique reference to the central tenets of Rousseau's
Social Contract reminds us that to relegate the suit to the status
of 'mere uniform' provides an insufficient and un-nuanced
account of its central importance in the story of European
modernization. In common with military uniform itself, with
which it shares a history,

it was part of a new delineation of public space, it
established distances, a code of human and social
relations, and was all the more persuasive in that it
developed an aesthetic.[7]

John Styles, in his illuminating study of plebeian dress in
eighteenth-century England, also notes the importance of
military uniforms, both in terms of their ubiquity (Britain was
at war for much of the period) and for their influence on everyday fashions and mores. Because British army uniforms were

paid for partly out of soldiers' wages, discharged men often retained elements of battlefield kit in their wardrobes, 'and consequently army uniform seeped into everyday dress'. Similarly, at moments when uniform was at its most extreme and elaborate, for example during the 1760s and '70s, when Prussian victories in the Seven Years War put the spotlight on the 'tight fit, erect posture and decorative accessories' of Prussian uniform, military styles gained popularity and inevitably were quickly copied by tailors or reflected in men's dress more generally as an aspect of self-presentation.[8] The brave British Grenadier and Jack Tar were increasingly providing the fashion inspiration for dashing men of taste.

But perhaps the smart flashiness of the soldier's get-up takes us only so far in understanding the evolution of the modern suit. While there is certainly a degree of equivalence and a tangible synergy between the military impulse to discipline, the practical affordances of uniformity and the development of a costume best suited to the new social and political contract, the showy ceremonial qualities of battlefield dress really represent a genre of clothing whose meaning was essentially martial in focus. Other forms of occupational uniform enjoyed a much closer relationship with the values embedded in Charles II's original invention.

John Styles and others have been persuasive in their suggestion that Nonconformist religious ideas and practices relating to plain dressing were more influential still on the greater prominence given to the simple suit in the masculine wardrobe at all levels of society. Quakers, who 'were required to avoid ornament and extravagance in dress' and 'placed a . . . stress on plainness and simplicity', issued the most 'thorough and precise' of sartorial regulations, informing their followers what was acceptable and demarcating 'the functional from the decorative, the necessary from the superfluous'. Quaker meetings were marked by discussions of troubling lapses into selfish fashionableness by wayward members. However, their numbers in the general British population were relatively small and their deliberately unadorned, outdated wardrobes, combined with their eccentrically egalitarian social habits, often made them figures of scorn or humour rather than emulation.[9]

The Methodists, led by John Wesley, enjoyed a much larger following, especially among working people, and their ideas on appearance adapted and popularized those of the Quakers. Wesley's *Advice to the People Called Methodists, with Regard to Dress* of 1760 offered specific guidelines for appropriate dressing:

> Buy no velvets, no silks, no fine linen, no superfluities,
> no mere ornaments, though ever so much in fashion.
> Wear nothing, though you have it already, which is of
> a glaring colour, or which is in any kind gay, glistering,
> showy; nothing made in the very height of fashion,
> nothing to attract the eyes of the bystanders . . .
> Neither do I advise men, to wear coloured waistcoats,
> shining stockings, glittering or costly buckles or
> buttons, either on their coats or on their sleeves.[10]

Wesley's advice was grounded in biblical direction and an anti-materialist world-view. Its words were intended to focus the observer's attention on charity and away from the distractions of worldly temptation. Importantly, it also provided a broader lexicon for interpreting and negotiating the dangerous terrain of sartorial manners that was decorous and 'proper', rather than ostentatious and vain. In that sense, although the homely virtues of plain dressing were perhaps taken up more avidly in the Nonconformist haven of North America (where they still thrive), in Britain, Europe and elsewhere Wesley's model provided a perfected context in which suit-wearing could develop and prosper.

It was not only the uniform cut and style of the developing European suit that lent its form so readily to military culture and Nonconformist religion (and vice versa), and thence to the values of society at large; it was also, at least with respect to Nonconformism, the suit's dark and restricted colour palette that increased its longevity and made it so appropriate as a symbol for the dominant concerns of nineteenth-century moral, philosophical and economic life that would follow. In his reflections on the persistence of black in the idealized male wardrobe from the Renaissance to the present, the literary historian John Harvey pays special attention to its importance as a marker of character and mood in the novels of Charles Dickens:

> The whole picture Dickens paints is of an England
> that has risen to massive wealth and international
> power, which is none the less a sombre place, run
> by men, and sometimes by women, who wear black
> often, and who . . . are frequently reserved, nervous
> and oppressed, however rich and powerful they may
> personally be.[11]

In the darkness of the industrial English city, Dickens's heroes and anti-heroes variously adopted the colour of death and seemed to impose, both on contemporary readers and on subsequent generations, a terrible sartorial and psychological burden:

> Dickens belonged to the world he described –
> a world he more and more depicted as inflicting on
> itself intimate injuries . . . he was not only the recorder
> but also a representative of a period when if black had
> the values of smartness, decency and respectability, it
> had also the values of oppressiveness and grief – of
> the mourning for something missing from the heart

Joseph Gurney, *The Sincere Quaker*, 1748, mezzotint. The Quaker proclaims his simple piety through the plainness of his appearance.

The alienating streets of the industrial city formed a fitting backdrop for modern dress. Here George Cruikshank provides an image of London for Charles Dickens's *Sketches by 'Boz'* (1837–9).

of man, of men – and beyond that again had also
the darkness of impulses, from sociability to sexual
love, constricted, distorted, and ready to rise in
murder. Which again is to say that black in the
nineteenth century has its affinity with ancient
black, and not only with mourning black, but that
it also has some tincture of a black fatality, of the
black that is of the Furies.[12]

All that darkness inevitably rubbed off on the man's suit
and its status in everyday life. In European cities, and in London
in particular, tailors and their clients worked hard to identify
an appropriate costume for the new professions thrown up by
empire, industry and commerce, one that communicated an
appropriate sense of respectability and responsibility. From the
1860s a combination of black morning and frock coats reaching to the knee and worn with straight wool trousers striped in
black and grey and a silk top hat was the favoured business costume of members of both houses of Parliament, city bankers
and stockbrokers, judges, barristers and medical doctors. The
fashion continued well into the twentieth century, until it ossi-
fied into a type of formal livery worn at Court presentations,
fashionable race meetings and society weddings and funerals
from the 1930s onwards.

At a lower rung on the social and professional ladder, the
dress of the office clerk presented alternative templates. Edgar
Allan Poe captured the clerk's presence on the streets of London
in his story 'The Man of the Crowd' of 1840. Older, senior
clerks from established businesses carried with them something of the austere character of Nonconformist dressing from
a generation before:

They were known by their coats and pantaloons of
black or brown, made to sit comfortably, with white

The black morning coat and top hat of the mid-Victorian gentleman seemed
to clothe a century in mourning for itself; *c.* 1875.

The tuxedo: the name comes from the dinner suit that was worn as
the informal dining wear at the Tuxedo Club, in Tuxedo, New York,
in the late 1880s.

cravats and waistcoats, broad solid-looking shoes, and thick hose or gaiters . . . I observed that they always removed or settled their hats with both hands, and wore watches with short gold chains of a substantial and ancient pattern. Theirs was the affectation of respectability.

Junior clerks from the 'flash houses' were recognizable by their

tight coats, bright boots, well-oiled hair, and supercilious lips. Setting aside a certain dapperness of carriage, which may be termed deskism for want of a better word, the manner of these persons seemed to me an exact facsimile of what had been the perfection of bon ton about twelve or eighteen months before. They wore the cast-off graces of the gentry.[13]

By the 1880s the jauntier costume of Poe's junior clerks had prevailed and the simple combination of short jacket, high waistcoat and tapered trousers, all in one textile pattern and worn with a bowler hat, constituted what was now commonly known as the lounge suit. In its more relaxed sense of modernity, the lounge found both a wider market and a more varied set of social connotations than morning dress. Since it was worn by everyone from tradesmen and clerks to clergymen, teachers and journalists, its neat smartness enjoyed a much longer historical trajectory, bequeathing subsequent generations the ubiquitous business suit of today. However, for some its associations, like those of the frock coat, still evoked a mournful and monotonous drabness that damned the materialistic impulses of an epoch. The lounge suit was a fitting costume for a creature that even the president of the National Union of Clerks caricatured as

a docile being, chiefly noticeable as the first hope of
suburbia at any time, and the last hope of the master
class during strikes. If he has given the world any
other impression than that of a professional Judas
for capitalism it is the vague idea that he has created
the demand for five a penny cigarettes . . . and guinea
Mackintoshes.[14]

Anticipating change in 1912, the Bond Street tailor H. Dennis
Bradley summed up the attitude of many of his Edwardian
contemporaries:

Surely, it is not logical to imagine that the present
century, which in general progress promises to make
the greatest strides in the history of the world, will
be content to continue the negative fashions and the
drab and dreary colours which are the legacy of a
century admittedly decadent in the art of dress. The
fashions of the men of the eighteenth century were,
from an artistic point of view, almost perfect. Why
then did they decay during the nineteenth century to
a degree of hideousness which was a positive offence
to the eye – to a retrograde ugliness without parallel
in any era? . . . The spirit and character of each age
is shown in its dress, and the spirit of the Victorian
era, despite its industrial progress, was sombre,
narrow, and deplorably inartistic. The tailors of the
day were unimaginative; they lacked creative art, and
their productions, in their endeavour to cater for
utility, lost all sense of symmetry and style.[15]

In nineteenth-century North America, the status of the
newly minted businessman and his suit enjoyed rather more
optimistic associations as a signifier of snappy progress. Yet

even in the New World the rapid changes symbolized by sharply pressed, ready-made clothes, polished shoes and bright-white detachable collars also brought a sense of ambivalence. The rush to profit, the rapid shift from rural to urban values, the erosion of social and sexual differentiation, the decline of meaningful physical labour and the reification of materialistic novelty favoured by the likes of clerks, administrators, shop-workers and financiers caused mixed emotions. Michael Zakim, a historian of New York's ready-made men's clothing industry in the period, captures very well the productive tension embed-ded in this new form of dressing:

> No more tangible expression could be found of
> the regularity – and notion of equivalence – these
> broker citizens sought to bring to the industrializing
> market and to the social relations growing up
> around it than the uniformity of their 'well broad-
> clothed' appearance. The monochromaticity of the
> dark suits and white linen of their single-priced
> 'business attire' constituted a capitalist aesthetic.
> It helped these individuals to recognize each other's
> 'utilitarian' fit as their own, and made every body
> a reproduction of the next one . . . They constituted
> an industrial spectacle that brought social order to
> an otherwise disordered situation . . . It was indeed
> a ready-made age.[16]

If the nineteenth-century clerk in his off-the-peg clothing was an unashamed neophile and a harbinger of modernity, the working man in his sturdy fustian offered a more timeless stereotype, but one that is nevertheless important in any con-sideration of the developing material and symbolic meanings of the suit. In many ways the manual labourer's rough attire has always stood in symbolic opposition to the ephemeral

Manual
labourers,
through necessity,
practicality and
choice, adopted
a wardrobe
that stood in
opposition
to the effete
tailoring of the
administrative
classes; *c.* 1900.

fashions of metropolitan life – and not always in a positive sense. Polemical writers on morality and poverty were drawn to the rags of the 'unwashed' as evidence of the supposed feck-lessness and wasted lives of their wearers. Samuel Pearson noted the tendency to slovenliness among working-class Englishmen in his prescriptive guide to manners of 1882:

> The working classes of England are far behind
> those of France in the matter of dress. In Normandy
> you meet with the neat, white, well starched cap;
> in Lancashire with a tawdry shawl . . . The men
> are worse. They never seem to change their working
> clothes when the day's work is over. Those who go
> to chapel and church have a black or dark suit for

55

Sunday wear, generally creased and often ill-fitting, but on other days it is seldom that you meet with a nicely dressed working man or working woman. I have seen political meetings attended by men who had taken no trouble to wash off the dirt of the day either from their faces or their clothes.[17]

The neglect of sartorial appearance was for many but a symptom of moral laziness and even criminality, and poverty was seen as no excuse for untidiness. But at the other extreme, the hard-wearing, functional suit of the working man also achieved a degree of rugged romanticism. In the context of an expanded trade-union and labour movement, fustian and moleskin could also suggest an anarchic and muscular authenticity that was thoroughly lacking in polished West End styles or emulative clerk-class dandyism. In a description of the attire of a working-class philosopher he encountered on Hampstead Heath one Whitsun holiday in the 1880s, the journalist James Greenwood produces a subversive vision that would have delighted even Edward Carpenter:

He was a broad-shouldered individual, attired in a moleskin suit such as is commonly worn by men engaged in the iron-working line of business, and to judge from his general aspect he might that morning have walked straight from the workshop to the spot where I discovered him. There was a slovenliness about his dress that suggested a studied contempt for appearances rather than a constitutional disregard for tidiness. His boots were unlaced, his waistcoat buttoned awry, and his black neckerchief, a mere wisp tied with a knot, was under his ear . . . 'You might think, seeing me as I am in my working clothes, that I haven't got any others to wear. You'd think wrong. I've got as good a

suit of clothes as a working man could wish to put on
his back – . . . made to measure. You won't catch me
encouraging the ready-made "merchant tailors" . . .
who grind the flesh off the bones of the sons and
daughters of toil, so that they may go rollicking about
in scarlet and fine linen . . . I've got a good West of
England coat and weskit, and I've got a pair of tweeds
that would stand alone almost on the score of quality;
but I'd scorn to wear 'em on a Bank Holiday . . . I'm
dead against the whole thing, from the sole of my foot
to the crown of my head, and if I wore a tall hat, instead
of a cap, blessed if I wouldn't brush it the wrong way.'[18]

Whatever their distinct political positions, Melton-clad
plutocrats, clerks in broadcloth and working-class revolu-
tionaries in moleskin alike found their sartorial allegiances
fundamentally challenged throughout the second decade of
the twentieth century. During the First World War men's bodies
were subject once again to the regulatory discipline of military
outfitters, often with the explicit intention of demarcating
social rank, while also seeming to subsume difference through
the visual and psychological effects of uniformity. Khaki was
everywhere on the home front, connoting simply a readiness to
fight and setting a dividing line between the civilian and military
worlds. Mass conscription ensured an imposed conformity in
male dress. Yet subtle coding still demarcated social and military
rank to those with the eye to recognize it.[19]

At the outset of war, officers recruited from the aristocracy
and upper classes adopted tailored khaki, cut by their bespoke
tailors according to the Dress Regulations for the Army of 1911
'as a lounge coat to the waist, very loose at the chest and shoulders, but fitted at the waist'. Within such regulations, the subtle
time-honoured understanding of taste, utility and personality
shared between tailor and client continued, such that Siegfried

Sassoon could record that 'ordering my uniform from Craven & Sons was quite enjoyable – almost like getting hunting clothes.'[20] Private volunteers from the lower-middle and working classes, however, were issued with much looser, standardized tunics of poor manufacture and a scratchy quality.

This social divide crumbled as the war continued and casualties rose inexorably, also creating a new terrain in which the language of men's clothing developed. The necessity of commissioning officers from outside the 'traditional' class of 'gentleman', and the increasing use of civilian volunteers and mass conscription, led to a greater sense of social mobility within the military, even while symbolic codes of gentlemanly distinction continued to inform martial practices, masculine appearances and social behaviour. The elite perfection of Savile Row-standard bespoke uniforms remained for those who could afford and appreciate them, but a more democratic understanding of military distinction was necessary for a new kind

As with civilian dress, the uniforms of commissioned officers during the First World War were informed by Savile Row standards.

Come Now

Your arms
uniform and
accoutrements
are ready
waiting for you

Lord Kitchener at Guildhall July 1915.

Be honest with yourself

The transition into military uniform for the majority of the British male population during the First World War had profound sartorial and psychological implications. Recruiting poster, 1915.

of modern army, and for the civilian contexts in which men continued to live their lives, on leave or after demobilization. In this way, elements of a new 'democratic' and 'modern' uniform permeated the promotion of masculine fashionableness and sartorial goods during and after the war, ensuring that practical, well-designed items such as the Burberry trench coat entered the everyday wardrobe and the popular imagination, breaking the elitist monopoly of the officer's tailor. War posters and propaganda started the job, but the modernist advertising techniques and imagery of the 1920s and '30s continued to prioritize images of the well-trained male body in tailoring that was almost classless, smartly functional, easy to duplicate, hygienic and suited to work and leisure, town and country.[21]

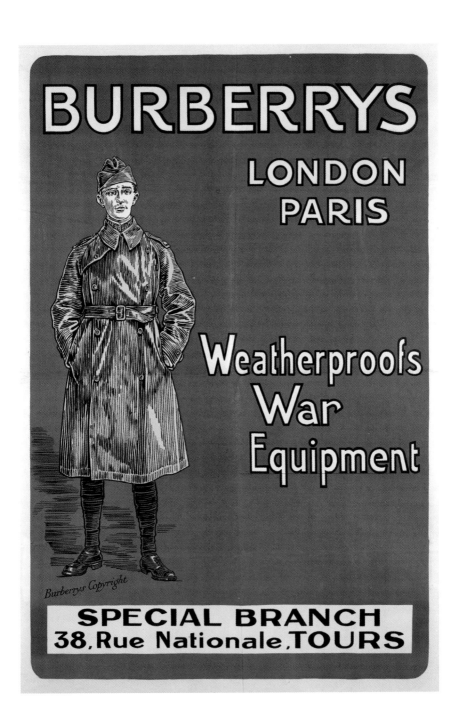

Some items, such as the Burberry trench coat, survived the war
and became staples of the civilian wardrobe; *c.* 1915.

Such trends were international, informed by American social values and marketing techniques as much as by the clean lines of European avant-garde design. In the high streets of Britain in particular, however, the resulting transformation, pioneered in retail terms by menswear magnates including Austin Reed (founded in 1900) and Montague Burton (who founded Burton in 1903), produced a consensual understanding of the suit as the defining badge of healthy and respectable masculinity – a *sine qua non* of the conventional – that survived almost intact from the 1920s to the 1960s. In terms of scale and influence, Burton was perhaps the most effective in pulling together military precision, moral rectitude and subtle taste in the manufacture of suits and the shaping of social attitudes: what the cultural historian Frank Mort has described as a 'reassuring image of collective cultural conformity – of a shared masculine culture fixed by retailing'.[22] Through the middle years of the twentieth century, it was the biggest producer and seller of menswear in the United Kingdom, and its clothing lines and advertising imagery, together with the atmosphere of its shops, promoted a gentlemanly ideal of extraordinary power:

> Burton's gentleman . . . acquired status by being absolutely normal. Neither spectacular nor bizarre, not a 'clothes crank' or an eccentric, he was secure in his personality . . . Burton's urged their salesmen to avoid dangerous items such as loud colours, 'sporty or semi-neglige attire', even soft collars . . . Burton's manly ideal was summed up in the company's famous memorandum to staff. All excess was to be avoided through restraint and quiet dignity: 'Avoid the severe style of the income-tax collector and the smooth tongue of the fortune teller. Cultivate the dignified style of the "Quaker tea blender", which is a happy medium.'[23]

J. C. Leyendecker's advertising images for shirtmaker Cluett, Peabody & Co. of New York captured the consumerist verve of early twentieth-century dandyism. *Saturday Evening Post*, October 1910.

Model No. 132
Medium Fitting
Double-Breasted Style
**The popular
two-button model**
*Back as shown unless
otherwise ordered*

Model No. 130
Medium Fitting Three-Button Style
A notch lapel model for business men
Back as shown unless otherwise ordered

Model No. 131
Medium Fitting Two-Button Style
Notch lapels feature this smart model
Back as shown unless otherwise ordered

Back of all models
on this Page
No Vent

In all positions of the new office life, the suit in every variation became the mark of the man, as in this American tailoring catalogue of the mid-twentieth century.

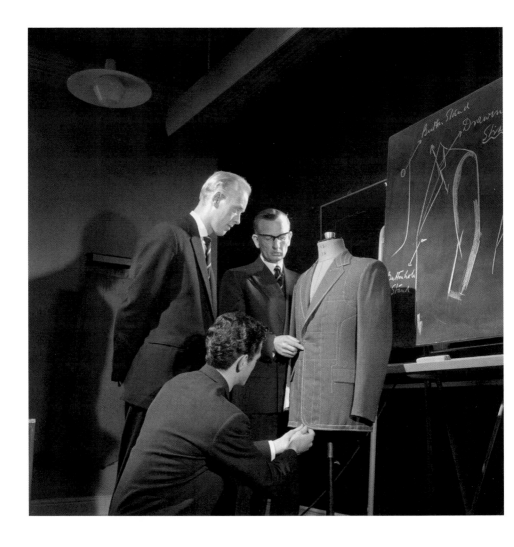

High-street tailor Montague Burton introduced the rhetoric of gentlemanly
tailoring into the sartorial repertoire of the suburban and middle-class consumer
in mid-twentieth-century Britain; *c.* 1960.

These were widely shared sentiments that inspired at least two generations of British men to dress in a manner that upheld the discipline associated with military uniform and religious observation. The moral and material traditions linked to the development of the suit seemed to have survived two world wars almost intact. Such reassurance encouraged the English couturier Hardy Amies (who was also an influential designer of menswear lines for the tailoring chain Hepworths, now Next) to wax lyrical on the enduring romance of the suit in his auto-biography of 1954:

> It seems to me that the basic principles of our way
> of life have not changed much. We still like to be ladies
> and gentlemen and if fewer succeed in so doing then
> at least more attempt it than would ever have dared to
> before. But all are fighting to preserve something they
> believe in. The young man who has just left his public
> school or University dresses, when in London, in
> a neat dark suit, with well pressed narrow trousers,
> cuffs to the sleeves of his jacket and possibly lapels
> to his waistcoat. Even if he doesn't indulge in such
> fashionable details, he would feel uncomfortable in
> anything other than a hard collar and a bowler hat.
> His more daring companions may flourish a flowered
> waistcoat and a velvet-collared coat, but if I mention
> too eccentric examples I may frighten the reader out
> of my argument. Let us agree, however, that the average
> young man of position tries to give an air of substance
> without being stodgy: of having time for the niceties
> of life. His appearance may be only demonstrating
> wishful thinking: that he has several thousand a year
> in the funds, and that income tax is only a shilling in
> the pound: that he is prepared to be a good father to
> a large family. But I think the wish is there alright.[24]

Hardy Amies for Harry Rosen, worsted suit in grey glen check,
1974. Tradition meets modernity in the English style.

Amies's passionate wish for the preservation of sartorial traditions was in some ways answered, for although the social revolutions and style innovations of the 1960s and '70s undoubtedly threatened the hegemony of the respectable suit, its symbolic associations continued to reverberate through the streets of both British and North American cities. In America the business suit enjoyed a revival buoyed by the success of John T. Molloy's famous books *Dress for Success* of 1975 and *The Woman's Dress for Success Book* of 1977. Molloy had worked as an image consultant for major u.s. companies and published a column on office style in the *Los Angeles Times*. In an era of Cold War paranoia and economic uncertainty, his mantra was essentially conservative, working against the freedoms of the counterculture in favour of 'scientific' market and situational research in 'real business situations', which revealed that men knew what was best for themselves in the choice of clothing, and that the 'classic' suit and tie were the ultimate in authority, or what would become known as 'power dressing'. For Molloy, men in smart suits achieved the competitive edge and gained all the prizes.[25]

The American influence on appropriate dressing for the office continued to the end of the twentieth century, although Molloy's business psychology model was tempered by a new emphasis on style. The noted fashion journalist G. Bruce Boyer published his popular guide to quality in menswear, *Elegance*, in 1985, and its fluid charcoal illustrations and witty anecdotes capture the flavour of an era epitomized by the ebullience of Wall Street and the confident tone of *Gentleman's Quarterly* and *Town & Country* magazines. Questions of taste and distinction now took priority over self-help hints on competitiveness:

> The business wardrobe is meant to comprise an
> interchangeable series of garments that allow for
> subtle variation and yet produce a discreet uniformity.

Too much color, too many patterns, or too discordant
a combination of elements in an ensemble acts like
too much wattage on a fuse box. If you plug in all
the appliances at the same time, you can expect to
overload the system.[26]

In London, writing in the society journal *Harper's and
Queen* in March 1977 (the year of Punk and the royal Silver
Jubilee), the style journalist Peter York also reprised Amies's
paean to the aspirational young man of the 1950s with his
description of 'Sloane Ranger Man', that upper-middle-class
reactionary whose confident self-presentation would set the
tone for City dressing for the remainder of the twentieth century. The individualist verve of his style could not have been
further from that of Molloy's results-driven clones, and in its
sharp ethnographical observation York's portrait adds local
colour to Boyer's more laissez-faire Big Apple approach:

I am in the San Martino in Walton Street with a
woman dress designer. Opposite us is a table of eight
very big boys. They all wear pin-striped navy-blue
suits, the trousers with turn-ups, narrow at the ankle
but loose around the seat, and Bengal-striped red or
blue and white shirts. Two of the striped shirts have
detachable white collars. The plumper, blander four
wear black Oxfords. These have specs and look like
lawyers. The other four wear Gucci loafers – the plain
kind, without the red and green ribbon. They march
across the floor, snap to attention, slap each other,
horse around.[27]

York's Sloane Rangers are indeed directly descended from the
military dandies of the Napoleonic Wars and Edgar Allan Poe's
men-about-town of the 1840s – all of them identifiable from the

From the mid-
1970s onwards,
the concept of
power dressing
informed the
structure of the
man's suit as
much as it did
working women's
wardrobes. Hugo
Boss, *c.* 1985.

As the City of London transformed itself into a global financial hub, so the dandified Sloane Ranger and Young Fogey of 1980s English folklore flew the flag for traditional tailoring; *c.* 1985.

military tenor of their bearing, their scrupulous attention to the details of the male wardrobe and their devotion to prankish horseplay. And if their showy demeanour lacked a little of the Methodist's reticence, it was nevertheless finely tuned to the religion of making money. Monetarism and financial deregulation, the neo-liberal dogma that would define the acquisitive tenor of political and fiscal discourse in Threadneedle and Wall streets during the 1980s and '90s, were less visible concepts in the mid-1970s, but the Sloane Rangers were in the vanguard of change, even if their fogeyism seemed to suggest the opposite. As York suggested: they

> talk about money all the time (but call other people who do vulgar). It's an orgasmic macho subject with them. However, they're shy of taking jobs in commerce . . . or in Industry . . . They go, above all[,] into the City. The magic words are Lloyds or a merchant bank . . . But the City is that much more competitive now than when their fathers went into it . . . Rangers now have problems with the job market. Their style works against them.[28]

It would be another eight years before the Big Bang opened up the City to all comers, in 1986, but already its complacent inhabitants were beginning to feel the heat of competition. Family connections and membership of the right club or regiment were no longer enough to guarantee a place on the board or trading floor, and incomers to lucrative City jobs achieved them on the basis of skill in the context of a rapidly globalizing knowledge economy, where strategic and technological brilliance, rather than the correct accent, were at a premium. The suit, however, remained a key indicator of the ability to 'fit in'. A City headhunter of the mid-1980s could claim, 'I'm not recruiting people who've merely got the taste to buy the right sort of stripy suit. They've got to be able to make money – a lot of money.'[29] But nobody yet claimed that the stripy suit was itself in decline. On the contrary, through the instability of the Lawson Boom of the late 1980s, the Exchange Rate Mechanism debacle of 1992 and the Barings scandal of 1994, the authority of good tailoring seemed to increase in value. Interviewed by the *Financial Times* in March 1993, the 43-year-old British director of a major European bank betrayed an acute self-consciousness and attention to form in his account of his consumption habits:

> On the whole, as I seem to be a standard size and I don't like spending a lot of money on what are, after all, my working overalls (I am keen on off-the-peg suits). I travel a lot and generally buy my suits at Brooks Brothers in New York where I pay somewhere between £300 and £350 a time. But I do own a couple of Hackett's ones which cost rather more but which I particularly like to wear when I want to look very English. I'm more particular about my shirts and ties. I buy my shirts from Crichton in Elizabeth Street – their shirts are very like pukka Jermyn Street ones . . . and if I want to look colourful [I wear] my Garrick Club tie . . . We have to be fairly sober-suited here so there isn't much room for flamboyance or innovation.[30]

All would seem to change again by the turn of the twenty-first century, however, when, informed by American management philosophy and the more laissez-faire non-hierarchical structures of a then booming 'dot.com' sector, many blue-chip companies appeared to relax their dress codes and encourage the adoption of 'smart-casual' outfits, while sponsoring such infamous schemes as 'dress-down Fridays'. A second leader in

The Times in September 2000 blustered characteristically about the effects of such sartorial casualization:

> The order of the suit has been given the order
> of the boot. According to a survey conducted
> by the London Chamber of Commerce, 'dress-
> down Friday' has triumphed, with nearly half
> Britain's workers marking the day by downing
> suits and slipping into something more comfort-
> able instead . . . Dress-down proponents contrast
> the freedom of casual clothes with the stuffy
> hierarchical reactionism of suit-wearing . . . Yet
> most dress-down directives offer no such licence.
> They carefully endorse the playing field look that
> is appropriate rather than the football ground attire
> that is not. If sartorial snobbery has really been cast
> aside why is it acceptable for a businessman to wear
> a polo shirt . . . but not a shiny football shirt . . .?
> The only difference is that a chukka is pukka, while
> business and football are supposed to mix only when
> confined to the hospitality lounge of the 'directors'
> box' (where surprise, surprise, a suit is the order
> of the day).[31]

The Times need not have worried. Chinos and polo shirts faced their own challenge eight years later, when on the cataclysmic bankruptcy of the financial services giant Lehman Brothers in September 2008, employees made suddenly redundant from their lucrative City jobs were shown on the television news programmes exiting the firm's headquarters with the ubiquitous cardboard boxes of personal possessions and overwhelmingly dressed in the familiar pastel colours of expensive sportswear. Nothing could have symbolized better a collapse in public trust of the private institutions in which they placed their mortgages, savings and pensions than the lack of a well-cut suit. For all its uniform conformity, here was an outfit that had been developed over centuries expressly to inspire confidence. Its apparent neglect had clearly been a short-sighted move, and prospects for the suit, as for the international banking system, seemed bleak.

It is perhaps apposite that in the first volume of his prescient study *Capital* (1867), Karl Marx chose to use a coat and a length of linen – the foundations of the clerk's uniform – as vehicles for a discussion of the relationship between the labour necessary for production, the use-value of commodities, and their fetishization in a bourgeois consumer society. Caroline Evans, along with other political and cultural theorists including Terrell Carver and Peter Stallybrass, has recognized the enduring relevance of Marx's discussion of the coat in the confused milieu of a postmodern, post-industrial, post-crash world. She offers up his complex, and arguably flawed, equations as evidence both of an imbalance of values in a dehumanized epoch, and of a plea for a return to materialist certainties. The coat (for which read suit) embodies the entirety of this spectrum in its stuff, its making, its acquisition and its wearing:

> Marx circles around the coat, the linen, tailoring
> and weaving, in such dizzying terms, at such length
> and in such detail, that in his narrative the commodity
> begins to assume a life of its own . . . [He] goes on
> to argue that both coat and linen could be expressed
> in many different ways: analysed for their use value,
> expressed as chemical equations, or described in
> their physical formation. Then Marx translates
> them into their equivalents in tea, coffee, corn and
> gold . . . The reality does not compute but the idea
> is true. And at the end of his chapter, Marx finally

introduces a gold-standard by which to measure all commodities: money.[32]

'All that is solid melts into air', as Marx foresaw in the *Communist Manifesto* in 1848. And in the disappearance of the suit from corporate life we are tempted to see a corollary. Yet in its very solidity, the ghost of the suit endures. Evans evokes Stallybrass's reference to the nineteenth-century clothing-trade practice of naming the wrinkles in a coat's elbow 'memories'. As Stallybrass observes,

> the wrinkles record the body that inhabited the garment, but to the pawnbroker every wrinkle . . . devalued the commodity . . . memories were thus inscribed for the poor within objects that were haunted by loss. For the objects were in a constant state of being-about-to-disappear.[33]

While the socialist reformer Edward Carpenter longed for such an eventuality, the commodity brokers of Lehman Brothers surely mourned the suit's passing. Neither could escape its presence as a foundational 'idea' of modern society in the industrialized West.

TWO

Suiting Nations

The fashion designer Hardy Amies wrote his pocket guide to sartorial manners, *The Englishman's Suit*, at the end of the twentieth century and in the twilight of his career as Great Britain's senior tailor and royal couturier. It is full of the blithe assurances, gossip and eccentricity that are associated with a creative generation who came to maturity in the late 1920s, fought in the Second World War and established their reputations in the 1950s. It also betrays the prejudices and frustrations of a class who felt they had experienced the decline and break-up of the British Empire, the damaging effects of social and sexual revolutions, and a world grown both smaller and less comprehensible. For Amies the Englishman's suit bore the weight of all those hopes and anxieties, establishing itself as a bulwark against the rude incursions of postmodernity:

> As a young man I lived and worked in France and Germany and carefully learned to speak French and German. I came to London and learned to speak the English of the upper classes. For twenty years my work has allowed me a flat in New York. From there work has spread into Australia and Japan. I go to these countries . . . with no more mental disturbance than I feel when going to Paris. I feel I know the size of the world very well . . . I want not less class but more class. In *Who's Who* . . . there are listed 28,000

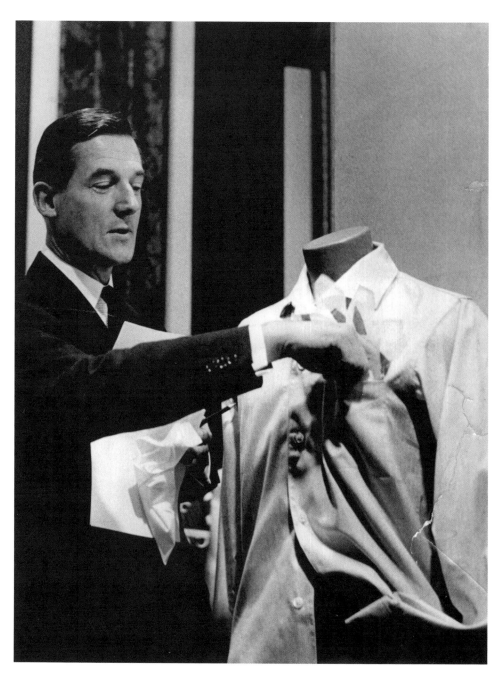

Hardy Amies, 1958.

Well-bred, comfortable and timeless, by the mid-1950s the Englishman's suit had come to signify the reserved stoicism of a nation whose imperial glories lay far into its past.

names . . . of living people of distinction – of class.
May their number increase. May their children be
taught . . . history, particularly of their country.
May they be shown taste . . . in gardens; in houses;
in food. May they respect kindness and order. May
they continue to wear a suit when 'class' is required
. . . We may have become poorer and given away
an Empire. But we still have an honest and elegant
approach to living. We have a social structure
crowned . . . by a . . . Queen who, in a totally
well-bred, upper-class way[,] has a calm view
of the vagaries of fashion and of the behaviour
of some of her family. The men of her family wear
suits when on duty, which is almost always.[1]

It would be churlish to challenge Amies's faith in the power
of tailoring to turn back time, but contesting the premise of his
prose also produces another history; one in which the Englishman's suit is positioned not so much as the prime achievement
of a superior civilization (along with gardens, country houses and
a benign monarchy), but as a much more fluid idea in a network
of relationships that were cosmopolitan, geographically dis-
persed and historically complex. This chapter, with due respect,
consigns Amies's Englishman's suit to the mothballs of a redundant imperial subjectivity and looks for its equivalents and
discontents elsewhere.

Samuel Pepys, another Englishman of reputation and a keen
commentator on the politics of the Englishman's wardrobe, in
reflecting on his own sartorial get-up offers an interesting
corrective to Amies's 'Little Englander' perspective. At the
beginning of July 1661, enjoying all the optimism of a London
summer soon after the restoration of Charles II to the throne,
Pepys indulged in one of his frequent shopping sprees:

Samuel Pepys in a hired silk gown. John Hayls, 1666, oil on canvas.

The epitome of cosmopolitan taste, Boston merchant Joseph
Sherburne, importer of exotic goods, poses for John Singleton
Copley, *c.* 1767–70, oil on canvas.

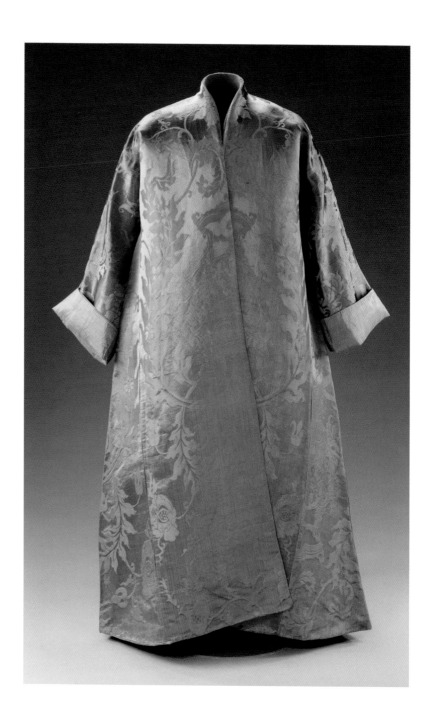

Silk damask banyan, *c.* 1720–50.

This morning I went up and down into the city to
buy several things, as I have lately done for my house.
Among other things a fair chest of drawers for my
chamber, and another Indian gown for myself. The
first cost me 33s., the other 34s. Home and dined
there, and Theodore Goodgroome, my singing master
with me, and then to our singing. And after that to
the office and then home.[2]

As a rising man of substance, with a fine job as officer of
the Naval Board, Pepys in his choices reminds us eloquently of
the performative pretensions of Englishmen's consuming habits,
which in some details echo through the centuries to Amies's
own: the elegant furniture for the study, the convivial singing
lessons and – combining the elements of quality, usefulness,
novelty, luxury and not a little theatricality – the 'Indian gown'.
Pepys was a worldly and sophisticated man, and in the purchase
of an Indian gown he put his character on show (at least to his
intimates, for unlike the nascent suit, such gowns were generally
restricted to the home or bathhouse). Five years later he hired
another, perhaps more sumptuous and fittingly patrician (this
time in Chinese silk), 'to be drawn in' for his portrait by the
painter John Hayls.[3] Pepys was clearly well aware of the cachet
that rare and glamorous fashions might bestow, and his auspi-
cious acquisitions set the tone for three centuries of dressing up
by Englishmen. For example, following his lead, it is instructive
to note the continuing play on contrasts between formal suit
and relaxed dressing robe through the nineteenth and twentieth
centuries by real and fictional British men from Robert Louis
Stevenson and Sherlock Holmes to Sacheverell Sitwell, Noël
Coward and W. Somerset Maugham.

In some ways, then, the adoption of the loose, decorative
dressing gown or 'banyan' in the seventeenth century stands as
an important foil to and context for the rise of the suit. As we

have seen, historians of male dress and English politics have generally looked to the 1660s and the Restoration for evidence of the prototypical Englishman's suit: woollen, plain, dark, symbolizing a new patrician sobriety in governance, philosophy and matters sartorial, and associated with the distinctive economy, landscape and social attitudes of an emerging British nation. But Pepys's Indian robe provides a counter-story in which the dominant narratives of aristocratic English taste are shot through with references to a world beyond the boundaries of Albion.

As Amies's reflections demonstrate, accounts of 'classic' English clothing taste have generally emphasized its innate conservatism and its opposition to ostentatious 'cosmopolitan' and 'urban' registers of style. And they have often confined themselves to the language of the suit. In 1948 the great English fashion journalist Alison Settle suggested that 'it is probably the un-self-consciousness of English fashion which is its most enduring characteristic.' She believed that this was derived from the stability of traditional English lifestyles, a world 'largely of men's activities, of sport, the love of animals, of the open air, and always of the home and its comforts'.[4]

This is a nostalgic interpretation, which has endured remarkably well. In 1996 the style commentator Peter York repeated the mantra in *Country Life*, that bible of the British landowning classes: 'Tradition', he stated, 'is what we're best at, and the dominance of tradition . . . is more marked now than at any time since the Second World War. Just see how those mainstream classics power on!'[5] His 'classics' included Jermyn Street shirts, the uniforms of guardsmen and cricket players, the Clarks desert boot and the Land Rover. Like the suit, these are all masculine icons that are seen to embody an easily identifiable English 'tone' (and yet which also carry with them histories of colonial and global connection).

Naturally, the danger of these traditionalist definitions of national style lies in their tendency to fix concepts of identity.

The lived experiences of ethnicity and nationhood as expressed through clothing and fashion are a far more contingent and layered affair than the rather constraining idea of the persistence of the English 'classic' might infer. Stuart Hall, one of the most influential contemporary writers on the challenges thrown up by conflicting definitions of culture, community and nation in Britain, stated at the end of the twentieth century:

> It should not be necessary to look, walk, feel,
> think, speak exactly like a paid-up member of the
> buttoned-up, stiff-upper-lipped, fully corseted and
> free-born Englishman, culturally to be accorded
> either the informal courtesy and respect of civil social
> intercourse or the rights of entitlement and citizenship
> . . . Since cultural diversity is increasingly the fact of
> the modern world, and ethnic absolutism a regressive
> feature of late modernity, the greatest danger now
> arises from forms of national identity which adopt
> closed versions of culture or community and refuse
> to engage with the difficult problems that arise with
> trying to live with difference.[6]

While one might debate with Hall on the historical development and literal existence of the mythical 'free-born Englishman' conjured up by his prose, his setting up of this narrow stereotype and embracing of a more open concept of diversity is apposite for any consideration of the cultural meanings of the suit and its evolution. For in both celebrating an engagement with other non-English patterns, forms and styles of clothing by many types of suit-wearing British men, and considering the importance of the suit in non-European cultures, we are at least liberated from the Anglocentric tendencies of certain forms of fashion history.

Britain's long colonial relationship with South Asia, for example, has had a significant influence on the traditions of suit construction, accessorizing and wear. And Pepys was not the first Englishman to engage with ideas of India through his choice of dress. Thirty years earlier, at a time when the craze for imported Indian textiles was generally confined to domestic rather than corporeal decoration, William Fielding, 1st Earl of Denbigh, had himself painted by Van Dyck out hunting with his turbaned pageboy, dressed in a glorious rose-pink silk shot through with gold-thread stripes, cut in the fashion of the Indian *paijama* and worn over a white linen shirt of English design. As a former Master of the Great Wardrobe and Gentleman of the Bedchamber in the courts of King James VI and I and King Charles I, he was no style virgin, but the portrait's inventive fusion of Eastern and Western motifs demonstrates a distinctive approach to self-fashioning that was in some ways much ahead of its time.[7] The traditional Indian trousers, tapered to the ankle and tied with a cord at the waist, would not become a staple of the British wardrobe (for day and night wear) until the middle of the nineteenth century; yet Fielding's pairing of them with a coat, modelled on the English doublet of the period but retaining a South Asian airiness, provides a striking premonition of the inevitable rise of the Englishman's suit at the court of Charles II: here emerging from the Mughal Court, rather than Whitehall.

By the beginning of the eighteenth century the British taste for Indian textiles had expanded across classes, but was more marked in women's clothing than in men's. Nevertheless, an idiosyncratic and subtle adoption of the fashion, as pioneered by men including Fielding and Pepys, persisted in combination with the suit in elite male clothing trends of the 1790s and the early nineteenth century. Waistcoats of the period show the ingenious incorporation of fine Indian textiles and embroidery. Delicate cashmere shawls of the type that were rapidly gaining favour among fashionable European women were sometimes restyled to form the basis of double-breasted jackets, the fringed

Some decades before Charles II's reform of court dress, William
Fielding, 1st Earl of Denbigh, had Van Dyck paint him in Indian
paijama, surely a foretaste of the two-piece suit, 1633, oil on canvas.

edge of the shawl forming the border of the lapels, which would have lain over the dark coat lapels in a highly romantic, indeed Byronic manner.[8]

A sense of opulent escapism also pervaded elements of everyday dressing for men throughout the 1840s and '50s in Britain, Europe and America, belying the notion that the suit brought only unremitting monotones and sobriety to the masculine wardrobe. Silk waistcoats were often embellished with Oriental motifs, from the ubiquitous *boteh* (or paisley leaf design) to swirling peacock feathers. However, it is notable that by the 1880s such extravagance was more often confined to garments designed, like Pepys's robes, for private spaces. Smoking jackets, caps and slippers, dressing gowns and pyjamas offered surfaces for expressive Indian designs that sat well amid the colonial clutter of gentlemen's studies and dressing rooms, but seemed inappropriate for wear beyond the comfort of home.[9]

When the fabric of Empire migrated to clothing for the public realm, its expressive forms were usually restricted to the merest hint of an embroidered waistcoat border, emerging beneath the dark grey serge of a morning suit. The tighter control over men's formal dress exerted through stricter sartorial and social rules in the second half of the nineteenth century might offer one explanation for the relegation of Indian motifs to the edges of the British gentleman's wardrobe. But it is also possible that a shift in the public understanding of Britain's relationship with its colonies, which followed the Indian Rebellion of 1857 and the naming of Queen Victoria as Empress of India in 1876, contributed to a more overt distinction between Western and Eastern fashion codes: between colonist and colonized. In this context the English gentleman's suit took on an authority that revealed the influence of theories of racial science and imperialist policies. By 1906, when George Sims published his magisterial three-volume survey of life in the Imperial capital, *Living London*, the division was explicit and spectacular. Count

Armfeldt's description of the 'Oriental' population for Sims's project vividly captures the approach, setting British reserve against foreign ebullience:

> Visions of palm trees and mango groves, of mosques and pagodas, rise in the imagination as one beholds the swarthy sons of the Orient, whose quaint costumes bring colour to the London streets, whose presence is emblematic of England's far-reaching commerce and power. The Maharaja who wears a diamond star, the Japanese who dress in solemn black, the Persian philosopher and the Parsee student one meets in the West End are all interesting figures . . . But . . . it is in the crowded thoroughfares leading

Traces of Empire regularly found their way into the Englishman's wardrobe, as in this incorporation of a cashmere shawl into a man's waistcoat, *c.* 1785–80.

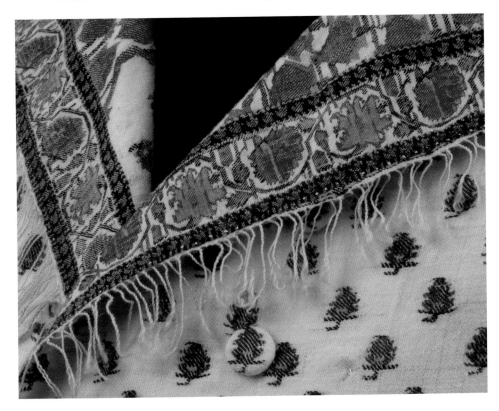

By the late nineteenth century, imperial opulence informed dress options that strayed beyond the confines of the gentleman's morning or lounge suit. Printed silk smoking suit, 1906.

to the docks . . . that one meets the most singular
and most picturesque types of eastern humanity
. . . The pale yellowish Chinaman from Peking who
almost trails his pigtail and whose loose flowing
robes are caught by the breeze, and whose soft thick
felt shoes glide silently through the streets, and his
brother from Canton . . . who wears sailor's clothes
and whose hair is neatly plaited round his head and
covered by a large golf cap . . . and the Cingalese,
whose figures are hid in long overcoats, and who
shiver with cold in the sun of an English summer,
can all be observed on the quays . . . and in the
favourite haunts of asiatics.[10]

From the heyday of Lord Curzon's Raj in the 1890s and
1900s to its end in 1947, Imperial dress codes also took on other
'exoticized' meanings in the British imagination. But it was
not just the skill and opulence of indigenous South Asian
crafts that were celebrated and co-opted into Englishmen's
wardrobes, or the spectacular otherness of foreign visitors that
was fetishized. Now the 'dashing' tropical kit and glittering
ceremonial uniforms of colonial adventurers and administrators were also imposed on the Indian subcontinent and other
outposts. Here was a colonialist's dream of pith helmets, puttees
and crisp cream-linen suits that lent flavour to the advertising
of Empire-manufactured goods and populated boys' comics,
romantic novels and stage and screen melodramas from the
1920s to the 1950s – even continuing to inspire British audiences
through the David Lean and Merchant Ivory film fantasies of
the 1980s and '90s.[11] In contrast to this, the burgeoning Indian
Nationalist movement, led by Mahatma Gandhi, promoted a
humble simplicity that set the pomp of the colonists in sharper
relief. As the historian Helen Callaway explains,

Doubts and tensions around the moral basis of imperialism often used sartorial tropes to highlight inequalities. Rudyard Kipling's poem 'Gunga Din' of 1892, about the sacrifice of an Indian servant for his British military master, was one of many examples that found their way into the popular consciousness, here captured in the 1939 film of the same title.

Gandhi subverted this symbolic authority by calling for Indians not only to return all honours and emblems granted to them by the imperial government, but also to dress in simple homespun peasant dress instead of the Western clothes or 'native' costumes decreed by the imperial rulers. The paradox of dress symbolism was exposed in the drama of nationalism: If the British dressed up in splendid uniforms to establish and maintain authority over the Indians, the nationalists dressed down to grasp back the power that had been wrested from them.[12]

Pandit Jawaharlal Nehru, the first prime minister of an independent India, developed Gandhi's creed of symbolic, non-violent disobedience through dress. But rather than adopt the oppositional loincloth of his mentor, Nehru and his compatriots

Sir Frank Swettenham, a colonial administrator in Edwardian
Malaysia, strikes the same swaggering pose as his seventeenth-
century forebears in tropical uniform, an icon of whiteness.
John Singer Sargent, 1904, oil on canvas.

Anti-imperialist movements in India and elsewhere saw political leaders adopting dress codes that either contested colonial hegemony or adapted it using local patterns. Here Pandit Nehru promotes the indigenous *sherwani* and Gandhi the *khadi* loincloth, in opposition to the British suit.

in the Indian National Congress fashioned the homespun *khadi* (undyed hand-spun cotton, produced as a challenge to the imposition of British machine-made cloth) into a tailored version of the Kashmiri *sherwani*, traditionally worn by prosperous merchants and court functionaries in the northern Muslim provinces. Refined through the 1940s and '50s, the 'closed neck coat' (*band gale ka* in Urdu) both rejected the English sartorial codes that would have dictated Nehru's wardrobe during his time as a student and trainee barrister in Cambridge and London in the early 1900s, and provided a material translation of his motto 'Unity in Diversity'. It is interesting to note that by the 1960s the Nehru jacket, as it had become popularly known in the West, had been reincorporated by modish designers including Pierre Cardin in Paris and Michael Fish and Dougie Millings in London, although the collarless, fashionably boxy form of their interpretations was a world away from the apparently timeless, light and elegant, knee-length garment worn by its inventor.

The search for forms of clothing that symbolized resistance to Western imperialism and materialism was not restricted to India. Perhaps the most compelling and effective sartorial challenge to the hegemony of the English suit as the uniform of political authority was the promotion of the 'Mao suit' and its variations in revolutionary China. The introduction of what was originally known as the *Zhongshan zhuang* in the early twentieth century – characterized by its blue, grey or olive-green khaki cotton or wool, five buttons, four symmetrically placed patch pockets and square-cut trousers – has generally been credited to Sun Yat-sen, 'the Father of Modern China' (Sun Zhongshan is Mandarin for Dr Sun Yat-sen). But its evolution was, naturally, a more complex affair. Its closest ancestor was the student suit or *qiling wenzhuang*, with its standing collar and matching pockets, whose military academy and school-uniform equivalents Sun had admired during his exile in

The classic 'Mao Suit' or *Zhongshan zhuang*, with its symbolic simplicity, evolved through the early twentieth century to become a key icon of communist China.

Japan in the 1890s. It was itself reminiscent of late nineteenth-century Prussian uniform, and enjoyed a longer history as the clothing of choice for Chinese ideologues and reformers. However, its form also owed something to the antecedents of pre-Republican Manchu dress types, the *qipao* (or cheongsam) and *changshan*, which had been used by the Qing Dynasty as a means of hierarchical sumptuary control. So its continuing adoption by civil servants and others well into the twentieth century could be viewed as a reactionary survival of imperial court traditions, as much as an attempt at progressive innovation.

Whatever its origins, Sun wore the *Zhongshan zhuang* intermittently from 1912, alongside Western-style suits and ties, elaborately braided military uniforms and the traditional long robes of the Chinese scholar. After 1915 his progressive marriage to Song Quingling, a sophisticated woman who had been educated in America and informed by ideas of Western modernity, must also have influenced Sun's attitude to the symbolism of contemporary dress.[13] But it was the circumstances of revolutionary struggle and international political cooperation that really informed his promotion of the suit. By 1923 Sun was in close contact with Comintern agents from Soviet Russia who were aiding the Revolution in China. The simplified suit he wore at this time, with its four patch pockets, bears a close stylistic relationship to the uniform of international Communism adopted by Lenin and worn by his embalmed body after its interment in 1924. So, in the year before his own death in 1925, Sun had become inextricably linked to the suit that came to bear his name, but which bore the imprint of widely ranging influences. Indeed, when he was buried in 1929, 'the Nationalist government ruled that all civil servants should wear the Sun Yat-sen suit as official dress, thus mirroring the appearance of their revolutionary father.'[14]

The succeeding regime of Chiang Kai-shek brought further modifications of traditional and modern dress in the struggle to represent a contested vision of the new China. The leader adopted a military style that was essentially an adaptation of the *Zhongshan zhuang*, but was worn with a leather belt, a holster and shoulder strap, and jodhpurs, boots and puttees. He also adopted its civilian version for high-profile events such as his meeting with Nehru in 1939, his signing of the United Nations Charter and his broadcast of Japan's surrender at the close of the Second World War. But the suit's communist associations always presented Chiang with a challenge, and it is significant that he adopted the traditional long gown for his meeting with Gandhi in 1942 and during the period of his defeat by and estrangement from the Communist leadership in the late 1940s: 'a wordless declaration of his allegiance to the ethics of China's past', according to the dress historian Verity Wilson. After 1949 and his exile to Taiwan, Chiang's habitual wearing of the

Before Mao Zedong co-opted the *Zhongshan zhuang*, Chiang Kai-shek (front left) promoted it as a national uniform in his role as leader of the Republic of China after 1928.

99

Zhongshan zhuang, with a dramatic velour fedora and elegant walking cane, was perhaps the ultimate rebuke to the suit's revised political meanings.[15]

But it was the modification of the *Zhongshan zhuang* for the Great Leader Mao Zedong by the master tailor Tian Atong of the Beijing Hong Du Clothing Company after 1956 that produced the standard version, known in the West as the 'Mao suit', with its wider, deeper collar and plain veneer, cleverly tailored by Tian for its elegant slimming effect and its suitability as the propagandistic costume for a personality cult with 800 million followers.[16] Mao's appropriation of the suit after Sun's death and during the struggles of the Long March in the mid-1930s also endowed it with mythic patriotic properties. Alongside its pioneer-like practicality and associations with a humble peasant lifestyle (its effete Western and Japanese antecedents conveniently forgotten), the four pockets represented the traditional Guanzi principles of propriety, justice, honesty and shame. The five front buttons suggested the five branches of communist government: legislation – supervision, examination, administration and jurisdiction – and the three cuff buttons recalled Sun's principles of nationalism, democracy and the people's livelihood.[17] The purity of the jacket's construction from a single piece of cloth echoed the unity and peacefulness of China, and thus its symbolic simplicity defied any possibility of dissent.

In the tightly controlled environment of post-war China, choice for ordinary men, women and children was restricted to inferior ill-fitting versions of the Mao suit: the *qingnian zhuang*, a simpler three-pocket variation for the young, and the *jun bianzhuang*, or casual army jacket, that denoted allegiance to Red Army values and the obliterating aims of the Cultural Revolution from 1966. By the 1970s the entire population of China had adopted these unremittingly practical and seemingly unchanging forms. The fashion writer Juan Juan Wu recalls that

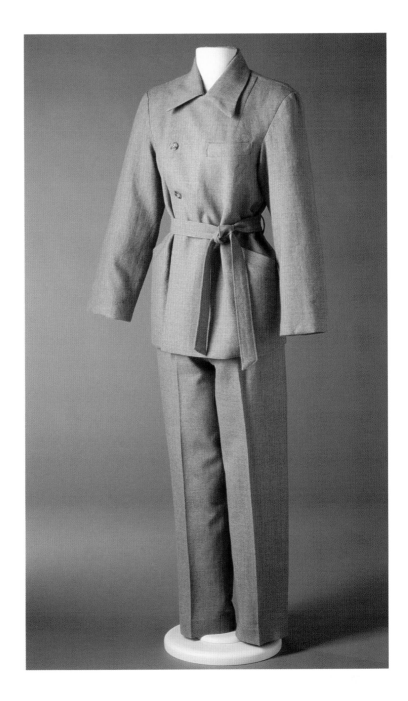

A practical, non-hierarchical form of working dress, promoted in propaganda films and posters, this wool suit was worn by women at the Communist Revolutionary base in Yenan.

The ubiquity of these plain, drab dress forms camouflaged differences in people's political backgrounds and views, and in a broader sense, mirrored the country's allegiance to the proletariat and the 'revolutionary masses'. In addition, the use of practical, simple designs and stain-resistant colours was an economic necessity in an era of scarce resources.[18]

The seeming erasure of cultural memory and personal individuality that the Mao suit aimed to encourage was, however, only superficial. Through its blankness, the ghosts of older forms of Chinese dress could still be discerned and future freedoms tentatively imagined. In the liberalized environment of Deng Xiaoping's China in the 1990s, Western-style suits and ties were increasingly worn by male leaders, and prominent women returned to the tailored dresses of their grandmothers. Now the Mao suit survives only in conservative military circles, in those nations still labouring under totalitarian quasi-Marxist regimes, and as an emasculated token of communist-era nostalgia. Verity Wilson notes its persistent presence in the iconic portrait of the Chairman from 1957 that still hangs in the Forbidden City, and remarks, chillingly, that 'within a crystal sarcophagus nearby, another of Mr Tian's suits shrouds the breathless corpse of the former ruler.'[19]

If Indian and Chinese versions of the suit were in many ways reactions against Western hegemony, growing out of local traditions but reincorporating Western tropes, the adoption and rising status of the man's suit in nineteenth- and twentieth-century Japan represented a far more harmonious fit, although distinctly dialectical in character. The rapid transformation of Japan from a feudal society to a modern one during the 1860s and '70s meant that its openness to the Enlightenment values enshrined in a sartorial grammar that had taken more than

Sun Yat-sen uniform, Hongdu collection, China Fashion Week, Beijing, March 2011. The *Zhongshan zhuang* survives into the twenty-first century, even in high-fashion interpretations produced for the contemporary Chinese consumer.

two hundred years to evolve in Europe was almost without boundaries. As the cultural historian Toby Slade suggests, the great wealth, inherent efficiency, absence of religious dogma, support for universal literacy and education, and embracing of urbanization and meritocratic government that characterized a self-reforming Meiji Japan all contributed to a shared understanding of the three-piece suit as 'a remarkable affirmation of a belief in a classical aesthetic and the first manifestation of what a new "modern" world would be capable of achieving through social and political rearrangement'.[20] In a sense, its sudden appearance in Japan was almost a ghost-like reiteration of its introduction in England in the late seventeenth century.

The take-up of the suit in Japan was aided by a longstanding cultural tendency to be fascinated with and immediately incorporate new and exotic styles, perhaps to be expected in a country that had always been geographically remote from external influence. This speedy absorption relied on the work of writers including Fukuzawa Yukichi, who travelled on diplomatic missions to Europe and America during the 1860s. His illustrated books *Conditions in the West* (1866) and *Western Clothing, Food and Homes* (1867) were hugely popular and introduced many Western concepts to an audience hungry for instruction. Their take-up inevitably produced many dissonances and mistranslations. Received ideas of Western tailoring were often applied too quickly, using inappropriate materials, colours and proportions that jarred with local traditions, tastes and even physiognomy. At the same time, Western prejudices reduced these rapid adoptions and amendments to stereotypes about the 'inferiority' of Japanese attempts at mimicry. But this sudden and wholesale shift to a new sartorial register became irreversibly real, and would have unsettling repercussions for twentieth-century constructions of Japanese nationhood and masculinity. Japan's political elite saw the introduction of the suit as just one essential element in a relentless and unforgiving race towards military, economic and moral superiority.[21]

But such changes also drew on local aesthetic traditions dating back to the early seventeenth century and the establishment of the cult of *iki* (elegance) in sophisticated Japanese circles. Encouraged in subtlety of taste by hierarchical sumptuary laws, the rising merchant class moved towards a celebration of chic that was observable only to the initiated and which prefigured in many ways the tenets of European dandyism in its 'less is more' dictums. As the historian Liza Dalby has put it,

> Iki was just as expensive as opulence, but it was not overt. How better to sidestep the stiff samurai who forbids you to wear gold-embroidered figured silk than to wear a dark-blue striped kosode of homely wild silk – but line it in gorgeous yellow patterned crepe . . . Growing out of the necessity to be discreet, iki made discretion its virtue. Yet it was a cool discretion, shunning the propriety of the established social order. The energy of iki lay in its streak of perversity.[22]

In 1872 the Meiji emperor decreed that Western-style military uniform or morning suits with frock coats and top hats constituted Court dress, and there followed similar strictures for formal and professional dressing that stipulated Prussian uniform for students and the lounge suit for clerical workers, businessmen and civil servants. This wholesale adoption of *yōfuku* (Western) clothing styles in the public sphere created its own tension and encouraged the sense of strangeness or perversity that underlay the perfection of *iki*. As the fashion historian Valerie Steele has noted, 'the very uniformity of Japanese society can provoke creative outbursts of individual style, as well as another style of creativity that manipulates the perimeters of uniformity itself.'[23] During the succeeding

The introduction of the European morning suit as court dress in Meiji-era
Japan produced striking contrasts with traditional Japanese clothing, as in
this representation of 1890. Toyohara Chikanobu, ink on paper.

Taishō, Shōwa and post-war eras, twentieth-century Japan maintained this fractured discourse with modernity and the nature of the suit. In the 1920s and '30s, *mobo* (a contracted form of the English words 'modern boy') and *moga* (modern girls) embraced the individualistic commercial freedom of department stores, cinema and fashion magazines with abandon, while social conservatives began to retreat into a pre-Meiji dream of nationalistic purity in which conforming to the aspirations of Western consumerism was considered decadent and weak. The release of sartorial energy that followed American occupation in the late 1940s propelled popular sentiment to the opposite extreme and resulted in the embracing of diverse subcultural forms, including a celebration of Ivy League dressing and Brooks Brothers elegance epitomized by the publication of Teruyoshi Hayashida's cultish *Take Ivy* in 1965. But a certain ambivalence remained over the rapid incorporation of foreign forms into the grammar of Japanese dress. The Miyuki tribe (those young men who adopted modish American East Coast styles) even suffered police harassment on account of their finely tuned taste.[24]

The inheritance of the Meiji restoration is visible in the degree to which the public display of status and character through dress in Japan still seems remarkably ordered, yet also unsettling to the outsider. The historian Robert Ross puts it very succinctly when he observes that the

> salary-man . . . will wear a dark suit, white shirt and conservative tie, the 'office lady' a 'prim company uniform' and even the gangsters will wear what amounts to a regulated dress – flashy suits and loud ties. Children, from the youngest age, go to school dressed in the livery of their establishment. More efficiently than anywhere else, perhaps, clothing has had its effect of disciplining the population, or at the very least of signalling the discipline of a well-organized society.[25]

The late twentieth-century Japanese 'salaryman's' allegiance to the
uniformity of the suit owes its inheritance to the regulatory cultures
of late nineteenth-century 'modernization'.

Yohji Yamamoto's austere, asymmetrical lines continue today, as seen here in his Autumn/Winter 2015 collection.

In a turn of events that almost brings events full circle, back to Pepys's purchase of a kimono-like Indian gown, a generation of Japanese designers who emerged in the 1970s and relocated to Paris reworked the concept of *iki* for a predominantly Western audience. Kenzo Takada, Rei Kawakubo and Yohji Yamamoto, among others, developed an austere creative register in which an obsession with 'darkness, poverty and asymmetry' produced the form and idea of the de-centred suit that in its ghostly insubstantiality almost seemed to shadow its more rigidly tailored and earth-bound European counterpart. Beloved of architects, avant-garde film directors and advertising moguls in the 1980s and '90s, the Japanese 'designer suit', worn ascetically with a crisp white shirt buttoned to the neck, proclaimed all the sophistication that Savile Row 'Englishness' lacked.

Across the globe, in a twist on post-colonialism that could not have been more different in substance from the ethereal asceticism of Japanese minimalism, the reappropriation of the tailored suit by the Société des Ambianceurs et des Personnes Elégantes and its followers the Sapeurs in the Republic of the Congo offers a colourful coda to the story of the suit's place in a history of empires. The dandified young men of Brazzaville and Kinshasa substituted the repressive French and Belgian imperialism, so horrifyingly represented in Joseph Conrad's novella *Heart of Darkness* (1899), with an ecstatic celebration of equality through the symbolism of dress. Inspired by the revolutionary ideas of André Matsoua in the 1930s and fuelled by the cosmopolitanism of African music and dance that thrived in the 1950s and '60s, returning émigrés from Paris fuelled a revival of La Sape's ideology in the 1980s and '90s. Now a familiar feature of popular culture throughout the world (appearing in pop videos, documentaries, fashion shoots and advertising campaigns), the vivid hues, extravagant accessorizing, extreme cut and bold gestures of the Sapeur's

The vibrant dandyism of the famous Sapeurs of the Republic of the Congo offers a contemporary riposte to the legacies of colonialism.

self-presentation are a proud rebuke to former exploitation and a confident assertion of aspirational style as ownership of the means to freedom. The (still incomplete) ten commandments of the Sape dictate:

1. You will be Sape with men on earth and God in heaven.
2. You will not sit down.
3. You will honour the Sape wherever you will be.
4. The roads of Sapology are impenetrable to he who does not know the trilogy of colours.
5. You will wear the ngaya, the mbendes, the tchidongo on earth, sea and sky.
6. You will maintain a strict hygiene with both clothes and body.

7. You will not be a racist, tribalist or discriminate.
8. You will not be violent or arrogant.
9. Still to be written.
10. Still to be written.[26]

THREE

Sharp Suits

In 1845, when the critic and novelist Jules Barbey d'Aurevilly published his influential treatise on the late English dandy George 'Beau' Brummell's approach to elegance as a philosophy for living, the subject of dandyism had come to represent much more than the simple matter of clothes:

> The trouble with Dandyism is that it is as difficult to describe as it is to define. People who see things from a narrow perspective have got it into their heads that it was above all a question of dress, of external elegance – that Dandies were merely dictators of fashion, bold and felicitous masters of the art of making one's toilet. It is most certainly that, but it is other things besides.[1]

In Scotland, Thomas Carlyle's extended essay 'Sartor Resartus' (The Tailor Retailored) of 1833 had already presented an ascetic critique of the solipsistic and inauthentic dandy stance as part of the author's wider reflection on the political, social and aesthetic economy of a rapidly industrializing and utilitarian world. Through the metaphor of tailoring and the language of the suit, Carlyle was able to present a manifesto for a rising Victorianism with its 'overt espousal of personal abstemiousness, social and individual improvement, hard work and earnest desire to be useful and do good', and all in the context of a great crisis in religious belief.[2]

The soft cut and flowing textiles of Armani's new suits favoured
male and female bodies through the 1980s and '90s.

In France, the essential function of dandyism as a revolutionary, performative assault on Ancien modes of thought and behaviour, as personified by Brummell and his circle in the confident new dawn of Regency London, had been translated into an exquisite discourse on artificiality and individualism for a generation of bohemians keen to retain a sense of aristocratic elitism as French society succumbed to the turmoil of the 1840s. Honoré de Balzac's aphoristic *Treatise on Elegant Living* of 1830 had set out the territory for Barbey with its insistence that 'clothing is at once a science, an art, a habit and a sentiment', its assertion that 'a man becomes rich; he is born elegant', and its dogmatic interpretation of dandyism as 'a heresy of elegant life'.[3] Charles Baudelaire's characterization of the dandy in *The Painter of Modern Life* (1863) saw the argument through to its decadent end. Here Carlyle's 'clothes-wearing man' had become 'the last spark of heroism' in a perceived wilderness of democracy and mediocrity. That elitist reserve and distinctively melancholic 'air of coldness' characterized a modern dandyism whose 'unshakeable determination not to be moved . . . [and] latent fire [which] chooses not to burst into flame' set a precedent for later generations of writers and artists who found in the dandy's elegant black suit and disdainful repose a dangerous amorality.[4]

By the end of the century the dandy creed had returned to its birthplace, via the corrupting influence of J. K. Huysmans's *Against Nature* of 1884 on English aesthetes. In London the literary and corporeal posturing of Oscar Wilde and Max Beerbohm in the 1880s and '90s repositioned questions of sartorialism, taste and ethics at the heart of the discourse of dandyism and modernity. It was the particular link they drew between sexual identity, class and the flamboyant manipulation of dress for men and women that invested dandyism with new connotations for the twentieth century and pulled it back into the ambivalent commercial realm of fashion, glamour and celebrity from which it had evolved.[5] How did the suit become a vessel for some of these debates, developing over the course of the twentieth century into a costume for rebellion? The simple lines of this counter-cultural tool and eroticized object of desire have found themselves requisitioned for a number of oppositional purposes. Some suit wearers, far from dressing to conform to the hegemonic demands set out in earlier chapters of this book, have instead chosen to use the suit as a weapon of style. In the spirit of dandyism, those who inhabit spaces beyond the patriarchal centre (including women, ethnic minorities, gay men and criminals) have incorporated and adapted the uniform of power as a vehicle for dissidence and disruption.

From the first moment of the modern suit's introduction as a badge of conformity at Court and in business, the dress and appearance of men whose behaviour marked them out from the crowd were adapting to different codes. Historians of sexuality have identified the late seventeenth and early eighteenth centuries as a pivotal period of transition from the prohibition of same-gender sexual relationships as a form of immorality, but not one confined to particular groups or indicative of fixed proclivities, to the more directed condemnation of distinct social types, whose transgressive behaviour and innate identity were tied to the homosexual act.[6] The emergence of what we might now refer to as queer subcultures coincided with the flowering of metropolitan culture in European cities, and drew specifically on the intensified and gender-specific fashion codes that characterized their modernity.

Thus after about 1700 the behaviour of men who were attracted to men was increasingly constructed (by the Church, the law and society) as depraved and associated with self-identified, often 'effeminate' types, not necessarily from the same social background. They were best known because of raids on the all-male brothels (known in England as molly houses, 'molly' being a slang term of the time referring to effeminate

A 'beau' of 1700 re-imagined from the perspective of 1791. Writers on fashion and manners were fascinated by the genealogy of dandyism over the course of the eighteenth century.

or homosexual men) that formed the focus for social and sexual interaction, and were often characterized sartorially through their extravagant rituals of cross-dressing and their parodying of mainstream marriage ceremonies and relationships.[7] Elsewhere, and particularly in aristocratic society, the licentious sexual behaviour of elites who might in earlier generations have enjoyed indiscriminate liaisons across gender boundaries without falling prey to stereotyping as 'deviant' was finding itself described in new, more condemnatory ways – constrained both by dangerous association with the criminalized identity of the Molly and by the pressure to conform to 'genteel' notions of domesticity and respectability enforced by the growing cultural clout of the mercantile classes. The sober suit, in this context, signified adherence to the rules and values of the mainstream.

The disruptive figure of the 'fop', fashionable, mannered and exquisitely dressed in luxurious accessories, represented an unthreatening comic manifestation of many of these concerns in caricatures, novels and plays of the early eighteenth century. In Thomas Baker's play *Tunbridge Walks* of 1703, the fop character Maiden confesses: 'I never keep company with lewd rakes that go to nasty taverns, talk smuttily and get fuddl'd, but visit the ladies and drink tea and chocolate.'[8] Caught between old-style carousing and modish gentility, the fop existed in a liminal space, between categories, but it seems clear that by the 1730s his affectations and contrived magnificence were increasingly becoming associated with deviance. Set against the new codes of manliness that demanded unobtrusive dress, restrained etiquette, handshakes and bows on greeting rather than kisses, and serious conversation, the fop drew attention for his 'otherness'. Tobias Smollett paints a vivid picture of the type in his description of the 'effeminate' sea captain Whiffle in his novel *The Adventures of Roderick Random* of 1748:

A tall, thin, young man, [wearing] a white hat,
garnished with a red feather, [his hair] in ringlets,
tied behind with a ribbon. His coat, consisting of
pink-coloured silk lined with white, by the elegance
of the cut retired backward, as it were to discover
a white satin waistcoat embroidered with gold,
unbuttoned at the upper part to display a brooch
set with garnets, that glittered in the breast of his
shirt, which was of the finest cambric . . . The knees
of his crimson velvet breeches scarcely descended so
low as to meet his silk stockings, which rose without
spot or wrinkle on his meagre legs, from shoes of
blue Meroquin, studded with diamond buckles, that
flamed forth rivals to the sun![9]

Whiffle's costume is a remarkably close precedent for the
transgressive dress associated with the Macaroni craze of the
early 1770s. This was a London style captured in the prints of
Matthew and Mary Darly and others, and associated at first
with the political circle of Charles James Fox. The effete postures and extreme attire of the men depicted were presented
in such a way as to provoke condemnation, and the wave of
Macaroni caricatures that filled London's print-shop windows
served to 'question the legitimacy of an aristocratic political
system and, at the same time[,] operated in the economic realm
as critiques of a particular mode of consumption that linked
luxury and effeminate masculinity to a lack of patriotism, and
therefore to a failure of cultural and political leadership'.[10] The
satirical publication *The Macaroni Jester* of 1773 provides a
clear description of the contested look:

His coat is very short and long waisted, with a fly
flap cut, leaving only pocket-room enough for a
handkerchief and snuff box. The sleeves are very

The return to sober colour and perfection in cut and accessorizing were defining qualities of the dandy's wardrobe.

In contrast to the dark suits of Nonconformists and patricians, fashionable young men were at liberty to select bright colours and luxurious silks for their wardrobes through the 1760s and '70s.

The Shuffling Macaroni, printed by Matthew Darly, April 1772.

low on the arm, and button close around the wrist. It is made so scanty over the breast as only to meet by means of two pairs of hooks and eyes . . . His waistcoat is out of all taste if not made remarkably short indeed . . . His breeches must be made of French black soy [silk], with buttons about as large as the head of a blanket-pin – they must come up close under the midriff . . . He must wear white or speckled silk stockings. Shoes buckled almost down to the toe . . . His hair must be full of powder and pomatum and the curls pasted close above the ear . . . And his hat must be very small and sharpened before like the bow of a Thames wherry . . . The fob of the breeches must contain a watch with a long gold chain loaded with trinkets . . . A long sword . . . must be tucked on the left hip, and a cane with a rich tassel must dangle from his right hand. He must have a large ring on his little finger . . . Thus equipped, he is fit for the park or the playhouse and all the world will allow that he cuts a figure – a-la-mode de macaroni.[11]

It would be misleading to read too much into an ultimately limited metropolitan phenomenon whose traces now exist largely in the realm of satire and reportage, but the sudden emergence of startlingly tight tailoring, bright colour and conspicuous accessorizing among a well-defined coterie of men, celebrated with a fascinated but repulsed intensity across different forms of popular culture, is highly suggestive of later subcultural fashion movements. It also forms a satisfyingly distorted mirror image of the dress and demeanour of those other contemporaneous Nonconformists, the Quakers and Methodists, whose austere approach to clothing set such a firm precedent for the modern suit. The Macaroni's stance was a prescient example of the way in which the trappings of material

Beau Brummell, first hero of the cult of dandyism;
from the book *The Beaux and the Dandies* (1910).

wealth and seemingly rigid sartorial codes could be subverted. In his world, suits could exist as templates for experimentation and defiance just as powerfully as they could be a focus for sobriety and duty.

Thirty years later the London print shops were full, once again, with obsessive representations of extreme fashionability among the city's young men, although by now 'Dandy' was the preferred term. George Bryan Brummel, known as Beau Brummell, latterly became the central figure of this revival, thanks to Barbey and other posthumous biographers. He was the paradigmatic dandy, although rarely identified in contemporary caricatures and until relatively recently a shadowy presence in terms of biographical fact.[12] Born in 1778, the son of the private secretary to sometime prime minister Lord North, he passed through Eton, Oxford and the ranks of the 10th Hussars to make his reputation synonymous with a new vision of the fashionable metropolitan lifestyle. From the moment of his retirement from the military in 1798 to his exile to Normandy as a disgraced debtor in 1816, Brummell attained a position of great social power in the circle of the Prince Regent, refining his appearance, connections and manners and ensuring that they set the highest standards of taste for the London elite. Some time just before Brummell's death in 1832, the young Barbey witnessed the shadow of this former style dictator emerge, syphilitic, soiled and delusional but still proud, from the door of the Hôtel d'Angleterre in Caen, and twelve years later felt compelled to reflect on the Great Dandy's rise and fall. Although Barbey warned against interpreting Brummell's story through the narrow lens of fashion, the centrality of dress to his self-invention and its subsequent co-option by writers on masculine style and purveyors of suits are inescapable.

The facts of Brummell's wardrobe are as fugitive as those that pertained to his life, but such is the paradoxical nature of dandyism. His first biographer, Captain W. Jesse, whose two-volume, then unpublished manuscript was of great assistance to Barbey, only recorded that

> his morning dress was similar to that of every other gentleman – Hessians [military boots decorated with a tassel below the knee] and pantaloons [pale, fine woollen trousers], or top-boots [black riding boots with a tan cuff] and buckskins [suede breeches], with a blue coat and a light or buff-coloured waistcoat . . . His dress of an evening was a blue coat and white waistcoat, black pantaloons which buttoned tight to the ankle, striped silk stockings, and opera hat.[13]

The occasional note of extravagance survives in such legends as his use of champagne as boot polish, or the ritualistic attention paid to the tying of his cravat, described in detail by Jesse:

> Brummell was one of the first who revived and improved a taste for dress amongst gentlemen; and his great innovation was effected upon neckcloths: they were then worn without stiffening of any kind, and bagged out in front, rucking up to the chin in a roll. To remedy this obvious awkwardness and inconvenience he used to have his slightly starched . . . The collar . . . was so large that before being folded down, it completely hid his neck and face, and the white neckcloth was at least a foot in height. The first coup d'archet was made with the shirt collar, which he then folded down to its proper size; and Brummell then standing before the glass with his chin poked up to the ceiling, by the gentle and gradual declension of his lower jaw, creased the cravat to reasonable dimensions, the form of each succeeding crease being perfected with the shirt.[14]

Thus there was perhaps an element of perfectionism, an attention to detail and a functional correctness in Brummell's dress that marked it out from the habits of others, but it was otherwise unremarkable. It was essentially through the confidence with which the man put the stark simplicity of his appearance on display that the distinctiveness of his sartorial behaviour emerged. His legacy in terms of the development of the suit lay more in the manner of its wearing than in its form.

That confidence was not only evidenced in front of the looking glass (and in public levées, where Brummell's toilette was performed in front of an invited audience). It emerged in all aspects of the dandy's life and, most importantly, in the broader context of the city. The memoirist Captain Gronow, once a neighbour of Brummell, recalled that

> in the zenith of his popularity he might be seen
> at the bay window of White's Club, surrounded
> by the lions of the day, laying down the law, and
> occasionally indulging in those witty remarks
> for which he was famous. His house in Chapel
> Street corresponded with his personal 'get up'; the
> furniture was in excellent taste, and the library
> contained the best works of the best authors . . .
> His canes, his snuff-boxes, his Sevres china, were
> exquisite; his horses and carriage were conspicuous
> for their excellence; and, in fact, the superior taste
> of a Brummell was discoverable in everything that
> belonged to him.[15]

A new metropolitan sensibility, focused on the dandy's body and the fetishistic impulses of luxury consumption, clearly influenced the transformation of the suit into a costume for posing in. Furthermore, in his subsequent manifestations (as Wildean aesthete, Bright Young Thing, New Edwardian and

The Dandy at his Dressing Table, c. 1818.

Mod), the dandy continued to refine a suit-based sartorialism that was configured to stand out, rather than blend in.

Oscar Wilde, the Irish playwright, author, progressive journalist, aesthete and social critic, was certainly much more than a clothes horse.[16] In both philosophical and material matters of dress, however, his unceasing concern with surface appearances and their affective power ensured that his own distinctive and constantly changing personal image provided a template that extended the Brummellian idea of the 'pose'. In the last three decades of the nineteenth century, Wilde did as much as anyone to challenge hegemonic ideas of the suit. From his admission to Magdalen College, Oxford, in 1874 he was clearly conscious of the effects of fashion. In early student photographs he appeared quite the student 'masher' in the loudly checked suits and bowler hats then associated with followers of horse-racing and the music hall. However, there was little here to indicate anything other than the keen following of trends. Wilde's epiphany came during his immersion in the ideas of Walter Pater and John Ruskin and his honing of an acute appreciation of classical and Renaissance art on visits to Greece and Italy. After graduating in 1878, he launched himself on to the London social and literary circuit, where he skilfully adapted the theories of Pater and Ruskin for a less erudite popular audience. His talent for self-promotion and communication soon earned him notoriety as the 'Professor of Aesthetics' in satirical publications such as *Punch*, where his long hair, loosely tied collars and quasi-Renaissance velvet suits challenged the mainstream sartorial taste of the time and drew the attention of caricaturists.

By 1881 Wilde's reputation was such that he found his opinions and appearance lampooned in the Gilbert and Sullivan operetta *Patience*, whose libretto ridiculed the current metropolitan craze for 'aesthetic' clothing, interior decoration and the appreciation of art. Turning this to his advantage, Wilde embarked on a promotional tour for the operetta in the United

States and Canada, dressed in extreme aesthetic garb – which now included breeches, stockings and pumps, fur-trimmed overcoats, cloaks and wide-brimmed hats. In line with the narrative thrust, Wilde assumed the pose of a 'pallid and thin young man, a haggard and lank young man, a greenery-yallery Grosvenor Gallery foot-in-the-grave young man'. The society photographer Napoleon Sarony immortalized it in a series of appropriately dramatic portraits whose sentimental bohemianism was a stark alternative to the suited status quo: the 'commonplace type with a stick and a pipe and a half-bred black and tan', to quote W. S. Gilbert's shorthand for the ubiquitous style of the British 'chap'.

Back in London, Wilde married Constance Lloyd in 1884 and set up a glamorous home with her in Chelsea. For the rest of the decade he enjoyed a successful career as an editor of the progressive magazine *The Woman's World*, while honing his talent as an essayist. During this time he exchanged the long locks and soft velvets of the *Patience* era for extravagant 'Neronian' curls (a subversive reference to the pagan moral code of imperial Rome) and urbane Savile Row tailoring (subtly accessorized with the notorious green carnation), the better to represent himself as the epitome of cosmopolitan sophistication and much closer to a Brummellian style of dandyism that emphasized a degree of elitism, ennui and, in the perfection of the cut of his suits, the distanced *froideur* of the critic.

By the late 1880s Wilde's exploration of homoerotic desire in his personal life and his work found resonance in both the amoral decadence of *The Picture of Dorian Gray* and *The Yellow Book* and an engagement with radical politics through his support of the ideas of William Morris. The publication of *The Soul of Man under Socialism* (1891) found sartorial reflection in the rational Liberty style of 'anti-fashion' dressing adopted by Constance and promoted through Wilde's journalism. Although his drawing-room comedies of the early 1890s set up a mirror to the mores and hypocrisy of fashionable London society and

Oscar Wilde in full aesthetic mode, photographed by Napoleon Sarony, 1882.

presented characters who were constrained by the straitjacket of suit-like propriety, Wilde's contribution to future thinking was much closer to Edward Carpenter's critique of respectability and hierarchy, which called for the abolition of restrictive contemporary clothing styles and indeed the whole concept of Western fashion. It led directly to the soft informality of the sporting flannels, Oxford bags and golfing sweaters embraced by the circle of Edward, Prince of Wales, after the First World War, the gentle, tweedy textures and tones of the suits worn by early twentieth-century Marxists, vegetarians, psychoanalysts and pacifists, and the campaigning calls for unisex skirts and bright colours sent out by the Men's Dress Reform Party of the 1930s.[17]

The tension between Wilde's public and private interests, indeed the dialectical energy of his dandyism, exploded in 1895 when the artist was sentenced to two years' imprisonment with hard labour for 'acts of gross indecency with other male persons'. Although the image of Wilde in convict's clothing illustrated a fitting costume for the final act of a drama that he himself might have written, he never fully recovered from the shame and physical discomfort caused by his punishment, and died a broken man in Paris in 1900. Following decades when his name, works and image were associated in the puritanical Anglo-Saxon world with 'unmentionable vices', Wilde's reputation was gradually restored from the 1950s. Sympathetic film treatments of his life and plays helped to bring his sparkling legacy to a new generation, and the counter-culture of the 1960s and '70s interpreted him as a sexual and aesthetic revolutionary. By the 1980s and '90s his complex personality and self-contradictory proclamations had made him once again the focus of intense study and speculation.

Some of that attention fell into the domain of queer studies, where Wilde's courageous and disruptive manipulation of surfaces was considered to be as provocative as anything that might have occurred in his bed.[18] As the cultural historian Maurizia Boscagli has suggested,

> the dandy's egotistic narcissism stood in open opposition to the chivalric virtues of self-sacrifice, courtesy, service, responsibility and work . . . it was the dandy's ineffectuality, his effeminacy and narcissistic otium, more than any sign of homoeroticism[,] that preoccupied and scandalized the middle class.[19]

In this sense Wilde's deftly stylized manipulation of his wardrobe can be bracketed with the energetic engagement of groups

Oxford bags, the voluminous trousers popular among British university students in the 1920s and '30s, were a refreshing example of oppositional style amid the conformism of middle-class menswear mores.

of young working-class men of his generation with shifting fashion codes and the new possibilities of ready-made clothes. Disenfranchised by the gentlemanly codes of the ruling classes or the self-policing of peer pressure, all manner of subalterns – from flash apprentices to street-gang members – found the expressive and oppositional possibilities of 'style' doubly attractive.[20] If the classic suit, inherited via royal regulation, military uniform and Nonconformist religion, represented conformity to a rigid model, the dandy and mass culture, in unholy alliance, created another, flashier version to set it in the shadows.[21]

No suit in the history of tailoring, perhaps, was flashier than the zoot suit, and no suit has been so divisive in terms of its reception.[22] Its origins lie in a number of American urban communities during the late 1930s, but common features included the seemingly extravagant use of fabric in its pleated and pegged trousers and wide-shouldered, long-skirted jackets, the vivid colour and use of print, the exaggerated accessorizing from brimmed hat and pomaded hair to tall collars and ostentatious jewellery, and the high cost. Young African Americans in Chicago claimed that Harold C. Fox, jazz band-leader and clothier, first popularized it as 'the end to all ends' (thus the Z), with its 'reat pleat, reave sleeve, ripe stripe, and drape shape'.[23] In Los Angeles its notoriety was more closely associated with young Mexican American men, particularly after the so-called Zoot Suit Riots of June 1943. There the suit took on negative racial and sexual connotations after u.s. servicemen led a number of violent attacks, sensationally reported in the press, on men sporting the look. Wearers were stripped and assaulted on the premise that attacks had been carried out on Anglo-American women, and the chaos escalated with counterattacks from both sides. The underlying sartorial symbolism was stark: to its detractors, the zoot suit signified depravity and decadence in time of war; to its supporters, it was a badge of defiance and community.[24] In an early iteration of the radical dandyism that

Cab Calloway, popular face of the outrageous zoot suit craze.

would come to define his public image, the race revolutionary Malcolm X chose the zoot's provocative drape as his own badge of difference, two decades before perfecting his own immaculate dress style:

> I dragged out the wildest suit in New York. This was 1943. The day I went down there, I costumed like an actor. With my wild Zoot suit I wore the yellow knob-toe shoes, and I frizzed my hair up into a reddish bush of conk.[25]

The zoot suit in its notoriety set a precedent for further subcultural twisting of the suit's inherent sobriety. In post-war London, its subversive possibilities played out across social class and for competing purposes. It appeared at first in the contrived New Edwardian style, a revivalist fad among ex-guardsmen and

The extreme elegance of the aristocratic New Edwardian style of the late 1940s and early '50s constituted a form of assertively reactionary dandyism in its own right.

aristocratic loafers that promoted formal Savile Row tailoring and whose bespoke wasp-waisted outlines set themselves against the baggy, democratic hang of the Utility and demob suits that served for the majority of the population. While the style's accessories – bowler hat, highly polished shoes and tightly rolled umbrella – provided a hint of the regimental glamour of the parade ground, velvet collars, embroidered waistcoats, ticket-pockets, covered buttons and turned-back cuffs recalled the recherché bonhomie of racetrack and music hall. As a look, it proclaimed its knowing elitism in the traditional language of Brummellian dandyism.[26]

Almost instantaneously, similar experimentation in dress, infused with some of the North American energy of the zoot suit, was noted in London's working-class districts, to the south and east. The compilers of the *Mass Observation Report* of 1949, recording juvenile delinquency in inner London slums, captured the connection between criminality and an emergent sense of what would come to constitute 'cool':

> Two youths, ages about 18, are standing outside
> a dairy. They pick up between them a large crate
> of empty milk bottles and throw them in the road,
> breaking all of them . . . They run . . . and join a
> gang . . . numbering about 15 or 16. Most of them
> are dressed very flashily – striped flannels and 'house
> coat' style of belted jacket; large, loosely knotted,
> plain coloured ties; and several of them are wearing
> the wide-brimmed American style of trilby.[27]

The favoured wardrobe of young men such as these, with its pinstripes, belted jackets, bright ties and extravagant hats, paid clear homage to the enduring style of the gangster film. It is interesting to note how international such styles were becoming, with each local iteration attracting moral panic in just the way the zoot suit had done in 1940s America. In Britain 'Teddy Boy' drapes evoked similar fears to the 'anti-socialist' short-and-narrow trousers and capacious jackets of jazz-loving Stiliaga in Cold War Russia, the former Czechoslovakia (where the name was Pasek), Hungary (Jampec) and Poland (Bikiniarz).[28] In Italy the garish suits of macho playboys were a similar provocation, injecting a dangerous glamour into the bourgeois milieu of Rome and Milan and firing the imagination of film directors including Fellini, Antonioni and Pasolini.[29]

The British Teddy Boy's draped suit evoked Americana and nostalgic music-hall glamour from the 1950s through to the 1970s; here Bill Haley fans sport the look at a concert in Harrogate, Yorkshire, 1979.

The particular Latin form of dandyism associated with post-war Italy is an important aspect of the history of the fashionable suit in the twentieth century, since it informed such localized traditions as those of the clean-cut American Ivy Leaguer, the dapper Parisian Minet and the sharp London Mod.[30]

Underpinning it was a sophisticated understanding by designers and consumers of the flexible social meaning of fashion, its relationship to shifting questions of distinction and identity, and its progressive ability to perform change. The curator and art historian Germano Celant suggests as much in his perceptive essay on the important Italian menswear designer Giorgio Armani:

> Fashion could not continue to affirm a social and economic split that at that time appeared quite visibly in its absolutizing differentiation, as witnessed in the films of that decade, from the garments of Roberto Capucci and Emilio Schuberth worn by the clerical and papal nobility in . . . Fellini's *La Dolce Vita* (1960), to the monochrome black of the upper bourgeoisie of Michelangelo Antonioni's *L'Avventura* (1960), to the motley and haphazard look of the proletarian class in Pasolini's *Accattone* (1961). Rather, fashion had to dissolve the distinctions, to reinvent clothing with a signic function that would become a surrogate identity.[31]

The film director Pier Paolo Pasolini's literary and cinematic work, most particularly his tender observations of the look of those displaced and hungry southern youths who came to seek work in the northern cities in the 1950s and early 1960s, is especially evocative in its description of the evolution of new, distinctive and influential forms of fashionable masculinity in the streetscapes of a modernizing Italy. The literary theorist Paola Colaiacomo is precise in her description of Pasolini's creative method, where

> the attention goes to the grain of the garment, its material and cut: a whole garment-world where levels of memory and desire hide and merge. On the one

hand the body is seen to strain the garment outwards, and stretch it almost to an extreme . . . On the other there is all the irrepressible flaunting of alterity in the new fetishes applied obsessively to the body in every possible way.[32]

In stories published between 1953 and 1975 Pasolini returned many times to the electrifying modernity and underlying violence of the proletarian Italian wardrobe. His striking words and images marked the emergence of an antithetical courtly style, where constant tension between American novelty and traditional values produced a bold, eroticized glamour that hovered between vulgarity and elegance, honed in a pointed shoe, a tight, bright white shirt, experimental hues and the ubiquitous ready-made two-piece suit:

Pier Paolo Pasolini's evocation of the rough glamour of southern Italian peasant masculinity, captured in films including *Accattone* of 1961, was a key inspiration for an evolving concept of post-war Italian fashion.

And then those clothes: those sickening clothes,
tied to the financial possibilities of the famous Fifties,
bought according to taste, a little plebeian, exactly
the style of those years: a sportscoat found in a
ready-to-wear shop. Of a strange little colour, a little
rust and a little orange, the shirt collar open, it too
bought ready made, in a little shop in the centre of
town; the trousers sagging slightly . . . worn and
a little short; the shoes eaten up on the outside by
the heels, like one who walks a little ape-like; and
especially those short, horrible socks, with those little
red dots, stretched by elastic a little over his ankles.[33]

These developments within the emerging iconography of post-war Italian menswear occurred within, and were synonymous with, the context of a radical restructuring of Italian society. The fruits of pan-European political activism in the late 1960s, a loosening of the tight hold on social mores traditionally enjoyed by the Catholic Church, widening access to education and employment, and rising standards of living caused by the 'second economic miracle' had pushed Italy beyond its agrarian, feudal past, into a present that found its meaning in a collective lifestyle dream. Nowhere was the effect of this new modernity more evident than in the cosmopolitan shopping streets, exhibition halls and design studios of Milan, the boutiques, restaurants and clubs of Rome, the beach playgrounds and villas of the Amalfi Coast and Sicily, and the glossily voyeuristic pages of paparazzi-fuelled celebrity magazines including *Oggi*, *Epoca* and latterly *L'Uomo Vogue*. Through all these the graceful figure of the new Italian dandy carved an elegant arc, but the ghosts of older versions remained present.

As the fashion historian Valerie Steele has remarked in her characterization of the resulting Italian 'look', tension has persisted between two opposing stylistic paradigms. The first favours an overblown, operatic celebration of life's pleasures and tragedies. It is a fiery carnivalesque tradition, infused with a kitsch nostalgia, rooted in the emotional psyche of the south and redolent of Pasolini's vagabonds and gigolos. The second takes refuge in the cooler refinement of an almost monastic simplicity. It favours the more abstract, anti-historicist pursuit of luxury for its own sake, restricts its influences to a philosophically informed, minimalist aesthetic, and draws its antecedents from the craft traditions of the northern tailor.[34] Intriguingly, Colaiacomo posits the idea of rags as the textile metaphor that links both paradigms and points towards the conceptualization of Italian fashion idioms through the form of the suit in the 1980s:

> As a type of clothing, rags belong to the world of the
> outlying *borgate* . . . In these districts, rags not only
> come into their own, but are forced to take sides. They
> mark both the final point of the evolution of textiles,
> and the steps in a very precise hierarchy. [As Pasolini
> notes,] 'The smell of tobacco, of clothes not changed
> for months (the same hard, caked trousers, which have
> taken on the shape of knees and the crotch, where they
> are worn and whiteish; they contain warmth, but at
> the same time a chill) . . .'. Ten more years will pass,
> while evolution prepares its next move. It will then
> be fashion which sends cast-offs, ethnic and exotic
> clothing from heaven: a cloud of 'soft, gentle rags',
> openly desirable and desired by all.[35]

Giorgio Armani's career has clearly followed the 'northern' route, and it is he who has perhaps done most to refine and disseminate a reconfigured understanding of the modern Italian dandy in an international context. Crossing disciplines from an education in medicine, he first worked in the fashion industry

The new Italian dandy made flesh by actor Marcello Mastroianni in Fellini's *La Dolce Vita* (1960).

as a menswear buyer for the Milanese department store La Rinescente, housed in an austerely authoritarian Novocento-style building of the late 1920s in the Piazza del Duomo. Its enlightened retailing policy embraced the new spirit of Italian design, reflecting the increasing affluence and discerning attitudes of its customers. In 1953, just before Armani started work there, the shop had hosted the exhibition 'The Aesthetic of the Product', showcasing innovation in domestic goods. This was followed by the sponsoring of an annual prize (the Compasso d'Oro) for the best Italian design of the year. Clearly inspired by the progressive strategies of his employer, Armani branched out from buying to work as a designer for the Cerruti group throughout the 1960s before establishing his own label in 1974.

Very conscious of the commercial need to accommo-date as broad a segment of the consuming public as possible, Armani developed a quietly unobtrusive sartorial register that

Giorgio Armani, reinventor of the Italian suit, 1989.

sat well in terms of a courtly insistence on a graceful persona. It also allowed him to market his brand internationally on a scale undreamed of by his predecessors. It entered the United States in 1980, and diversified to a younger, unisex clientele via the jeans- and sportswear-based Emporio Armani line from 1989. But to emphasize the business acumen of Armani at the expense of his impact on the development of the aesthetics of the male suit would be distorting. His disarming practicality belied an attention to function, form and finish that revolutionized the direction of fashion from the mid-1980s.

Armani famously eviscerated the structure of the formal business suit, sloping the shoulders, freeing the stiffened lining, lowering the buttons and lapels, and adopting fabrics that were lighter in weight, texture and colour. It was as if the traces of modernity present in the American Ivy League sack suit of the late 1950s and the rags of a common memory of post-war deprivation and aspiration in Italy had blurred together, producing a new, more timely elegance:

> Armani understood that clothing was . . . part of
> the everyday management of one's appearance, a
> tool of personal symbology: 'When I began to design,
> men all dressed in the same way. American industry
> called the shots, with its technicians scattered all over
> the world . . . all impeccably equal, equally impeccable
> . . . They had no defects. But I liked defect. I wanted to
> personalize the jacket, to make it more closely attuned
> to its wearer. How? By removing the structure. Making
> it into a sort of second skin.'[36]

Armani's invention of a 'second skin' signalled a new sense of femininity in the presentation of Italian men's clothing that was profoundly radicalizing; an abandonment, in the spirit of *sprezzatura*, to its tactile qualities, its soft, caressing feel on the

Richard Gere in powder-blue Armani for Paul Schrader's *American Gigolo* (1980).

body. At the same time the puritanical hold on a subtly differ-
entiated framework of restrained tones, textures and shades,
and a deliberate contrast with the hard surfaces of the muscular body shape fetishized in 1980s popular culture, produced a
frisson that Armani had begun to explore at the beginning of
the decade in his designs for Richard Gere's lead character,
Julian, in the film *American Gigolo*, directed by Paul Schrader.
In the famous dressing scene, Julian's playful toilette antici-
pates a new male narcissism that was to become the signature
of Italianate fashionability by the close of the decade:

> He selects things as though wanting to avoid and
> deflect attention, entrusting himself to a secret, silent
> acceptability in which sweetness and softness are the
> true protagonists of his seduction, which interweaves
> the virile and the feminine . . . He avails himself of a
> form of expression and a mask capable of mimicking
> – like his clothes and outer layer – the desire and
> pleasure of the other person. He thus avoids vulgarity
> and spectacle, dissolving the impetus and perfection
> of his limitlessly available body in the suppleness
> of the materials and colours that liberate its sensual
> form, but grant him, in their uniformity and measure,
> a triumphant innocence.[37]

Such innocent triumphalism should not, however, be taken
as evidence that a more overtly theatrical engagement with the
bacchanalian spirit of 'southern' sensibilities had been stifled.
Other Italian designers of Armani's generation produced
collections that made very different play with the idea of the
suit, creating versions that were in turn more libidinous, sensual and brashly glamorous. Walter Albini was one. Steeped
in the cinematic traditions of 1930s and '40s Hollywood, which
had informed his childhood dreams, he excelled in textile

design, fashion illustration and interior design, and began producing exotically themed womenswear for a number of Italian companies and boutiques in 1964. Between then and the early 1980s (he died in Milan in 1983), Albini's technically brilliant experiments with sinuous unisex and cartoon-like menswear collections were the high points of the Milanese fashion season, sharing much with the exuberantly camp but always chic aesthetic employed by his contemporaries elsewhere in Europe (among them Yves Saint Laurent and Ossie Clark). His heyday was perhaps the mid-1970s, when his deliberately nostalgic take on the 'Latin Lover' Riviera style of the 1920s was the quintessence of international good taste. As *Time* magazine recorded in the spring of 1973,

> For many designers and their customers, the 'In' echo
> is of the '20s – not so much of the roaring of the jazz
> babies in speakeasies as the tinkling of cocktail glasses
> on Long Island lawns and the rustle of silk against
> chiffon. In the U.S. the style is frequently called the
> Gatsby look, a catch phrase that doubtless will get a
> boost with the remake this year of a movie based on
> F. Scott Fitzgerald's novella. French magazines are calling
> it le style tennis or the Deauville look. But it might
> just as easily be described as the Newport-to-Palm
> Beach mood . . . or the Devereux Milburn look (for
> the '20s polo hero). Polo, tennis and golf – not as they
> were played but as they were watched – are central to
> the sporting-set concept . . . The idea is elegance – a
> calculatedly casual, languid elegance, suggesting an
> evanescent Fitzgerald memory of the summer of '22.
> 'To want to walk out on the lawn wearing a white silk
> shirt and white flannels presents a very rich dream-like
> atmosphere,' says New York designer Ralph Lauren
> . . . Milan's Walter Albini, who might be called the

Walter Albini's glamorous designs enjoyed an intense moment of appreciation by the international fashion set in the mid-1970s.

Godfather of the Italian Gatsby look, has drawn
on the Fitzgerald era since he first started designing
ten years ago. 'It was a cultural high-water mark in
fashion, decorating, literature, painting,' he contends.
'Actually, nobody has done anything new since . . .'[38]

Alongside Armani, Gianni Versace would prove the excep-
tion to Albini's claims of creative stasis, offering an exciting
and entirely innovative contribution to the evolution of Italian
menswear in the last quarter of the twentieth century. His unique
skill lay in his ability to translate the material outcomes of Italy's
cultural and economic transformation so that they met the
more diffuse desires of an international market, but in an idiom
radically different from Armani's transcendental modernism.
Trained as an architect in his native southern Italy, but raised
as a tailor in the domestic context of his mother's dressmaking
business, Versace developed an early and useful knowledge of
broader European fashion trends through his role as a buyer for
the family firm in Paris and London in the late 1960s. Between
then and 1978, when he established his eponymous business,
Versace worked as a designer for several of the small Milanese
companies whose rising fortunes were also changing the profile
of the city.[39] His own journey from an artisanal background in
the south to the sophisticated ambience of the north was one
that had been shared by many of his compatriots, and there is
something autobiographical in his mature work that paid passionate homage both to the idea of traditional roots in the
sensual primitivism of an older way of life and to the promise
of worldly success inherent in the consumerist, market-driven
tenets of the modern world; a luxurious materialism that was
entirely unapologetic and owed much to courtly traditions of
'magnificence'.[40]

Throughout the 1980s and '90s Versace pioneered a distinctively voluptuous signature style for men and women, using

extraordinarily rich fabrics and often aiming to emphasize the sexuality or social power of the wearer through cut and surface. Running alongside commissions for opera and ballet costumes from La Scala and the director/choreographer Maurice Béjart, his designs embraced a vivid theatricality and sense of occasion and were readily adopted by those in the film, sport and culture industries whose professional responsibilities demanded prominent public exposure (Sir Roy Strong, former director of the Victoria & Albert Museum in London, was an enthusiastic patron of Versace's work, and a wide selection of his Versace suits are now in the Fashion Museum in Bath).

From the clinging sinuousness of the metallic fabrics and sculpted leather employed in his collections of the early 1980s to the opulent Mannerist prints and glittering accessories that signalled glamour and expense in the 1990s, Versace's output made deliberate play with the overlapping categories of beauty and vulgarity. Under the aggressive business control of his brother Santo, the brand also functioned on two complementary levels. It came to be regarded as the chosen uniform of the new super-rich, sold at prohibitive prices in spectacular boutiques at the world's most exclusive locations, while through the wider marketing of fragrances, diffusion lines and, from 1993, home furnishings, it formed the paradoxical symbol of a more popular celebration of success, crystallized in the emergence of the ubiquitous celebrity culture.

In the trademark of the Medusa's head, which Versace adopted as his crest, the designer signalled his understanding of the sublime propensity of fashion to shock and horrify, but most importantly to awe the consumer into submission. His personal tastes and desires were photographed for a succession of promotional books and advertising campaigns that hymned the lush surfaces of his several palaces as though they were sets for a Visconti film, and lovingly described the bronzed bodies of his princely coterie (often depicted naked, but for the modest

Gianni Versace, purveyor of sensuality to the celebrity cultures of the late twentieth century, here in padded and pegged suit, 1981.

draping of a Versace tie). The imagery was deliberately intoxicating in its all-enveloping, sensual appeal, and left little room for subversion or alternative choices on the part of his intended audience. The meaning of the 'sharp' suit, in this sense, had by the turn of the century been blunted, stripped of its capacity to undermine the status quo, reduced to mere 'costume'.

The commercial clout of an organization that was enjoying a phenomenal turnover of £600 million and profits of £60 million in 1996 also had the effect of stifling dissent in the fashion media, ensuring maximum press coverage and adulation. But Versace's vision was, according to some critics, ultimately empty of any deeper meaning and quite terrifying in its aesthetic predictability – a veritable pornography of fashion, whose values seemed to bring it too close to that other cliché of Italian masculinity, the Mafiosi. The mythic status of the brand was only strengthened in 1997 when the designer was murdered on the steps of his Miami mansion. True to the family traditions on which the brand had been built, his legacy was taken up by his sister and muse Donatella, who continued to purvey the compelling Versace version of courtly glamour to twenty-first-century consumers with characteristic verve.

Something of this spirit can also be found persisting in the present decade through the enduring stereotype of the Italian playboy and his taste for the good things. In Naples, the modernizing traditions of tailoring establishments such as Cesare Attolini, Kiton and Rubinacci (most of them founded between 1930 and 1970) continue to draw heavily on their reputation for exacting and expensive craftsmanship, which appeals particularly to the conspicuous tastes of the new super-rich of Russia. It has certainly been a continuing and defining characteristic of more established northern brands, including the Roman luxury sportswear and accessories retailer Gucci from 1945 until today. The journalist Karin Nelson recalls:

Celebrities and aristocrats, in the spirit of post-war
liberation, filled Gucci's shop on via Condotti . . .
gentlemen like the actor Gigi Rizzi, whose most
enduring legacy was the women he wooed (Brigitte
Bardot, Verushka), and Walter Chiari, who had an
affair with Ava Gardner while she was still married
to Frank Sinatra. Handsome, well travelled, sexually
irresistible and impeccably turned out, these sorts of
fellows would come to represent not just a masculine
ideal, but an archetype of the Gucci male . . . The
beauty of playboys is that they never get old; rather
they are perpetually seductive.[41]

The ageless and seductive beauty of the Italian playboy
was perhaps an inspiration for the American designer Tom
Ford, who was taken on by Gucci as a womenswear designer
in 1990. The company was then struggling financially and
beset with scandal, but Ford rose swiftly through its ranks,
becoming design director in 1992 and creative director with
ultimate responsibility for the company's entire product range
and public image in 1994. From then until his departure in
2004, Ford 'was able to return the brand to the worldly prominence of its golden age, evoking memories of luxury and the
jet-set lifestyle'.[42] The signature components of the Ford/Gucci
look, culled from the experiences of a youth misspent in Studio
54 and a libidinous catalogue of sharp tailoring, lizard-skin
loafers, velvet smoking jackets, tightly caressing knitwear,
silk-jacquard ascots and amber-tinted aviator sunglasses that
directly reference a half-century of Mediterranean *sprezzatura*, mark something close to the apotheosis of an Italianate
masculine style that has become truly global and highly
consumerist. As impossible to pin down as the definition of
dandyism, and perhaps a shadow of its radical 1950s origins,
the evolving nature of the Italian suit has nevertheless left its

In his work for Gucci, American designer Tom Ford rejuvenated the idea of Italian luxury tailoring.

Tom Ford on the ubiquitous red carpet.

distinctive imprint on the self-presentation of sartorially aware men everywhere.

The co-option of a revolutionary dandyism has not been the preserve of men only. The sharpest suits, one might argue, have been those worn by women. Tailored garments fashioned for the needs of newly active women, but adapted from the cut of men's military and sporting costumes, had been a familiar part of the affluent Western woman's wardrobe since the 1860s (and could be traced further back, to the riding habits of the late seventeenth century). As Lou Taylor has noted,

> The tailoring techniques of cutting, shaping and making up such garments were very different from those of dressmakers working with silk, fine wool and cottons . . . Using heavy wool cloth, the specific skills of the expert tailor were required, such as cutting, fitting, interlining, wadding, stab stitching and the shaping and steaming of sewn cloth with heavy heated irons and so on. At the same time, the tailor still had to take care that his styles responded to the established etiquette codes of the period in order that they should be acceptable to his . . . conventional clients.[43]

The appropriation of tweed, tartan and braided frogging for women's walking and climbing suits, ulster raincoats and travelling ensembles, and the diversification of staid Savile Row tailors into the female market, was not in itself an affront to convention.[44] The shock lay in the readiness of some women, unconstrained by etiquette or society, to take the development further and adopt masculine styles, not for reasons of disguise (there is a long tradition of extraordinary women 'passing' as men in the army and navy, for example) or functional ease (the better to raise a croquet hammer or push on a bicycle pedal), but as a means of asserting a counter-cultural identity and deriving

Hardy Amies, woman's suit.

Radclyffe Hall, author of the novel of lesbian love *The Well of Loneliness* (1928) and pioneer of the tailored look for women.

pleasure from the resulting dissonance. Artists, women who
loved women, performers and the ultra-fashionable or demi-
monde were unsatisfied with the partial strengthening of seams
and thickening of fabric that the adoption of 'tailored' styles
offered. Their interest was in the wholesale translation of the
man's suit as an object refitted for the female body and transformed by her desire. The high-profile 'cross-dressing' of Mary
Walker, George Sand, Una, Lady Troubridge, Hannah Gluckstein,
Violet Trefusis, Colette and Marlene Dietrich into either the
working man's loungewear or the aristocrat's eveningwear punc-
tuated the nineteenth and early twentieth centuries with an
erotic charge that scandalized and titillated respectable society
in equal measure.[45] For the women themselves the effect was
profound. In fact, in some sense it could be argued that the
male suit produced the image of the modern lesbian, allowing
her to play with the fixed meanings of body, clothing and sexual
orientation, disrupting the accepted, patriarchal understanding of all three to create something radical and empowering.[46]

The fascinating queerness of the suited woman was not lost
on mainstream popular culture, where it was rapidly digested
for wider consumption. On the music-hall stage of the 1890s
and 1900s, the male impersonator offered an unsettling critique,
both of young men's propensity to fashionable pretension and
of the mirage of gender sustained by the performative possibilities of the suit. One of the best of them, Vesta Tilley, refined
such sartorial fetishism into a commercial art form. Recalling
a tour of the United States, she noted:

> The dudes of Broadway were intrigued with my
> costume, a pearl grey frock coat suit and silk hat
> and a vest of delicately flowered silk – one of the dozens
> which I had bought at the sale of the effects of the late
> Marquis of Anglesey. Grey frock suits and fancy vests
> became very popular in New York . . . All my male

costumes were absolutely the latest in fashionable men's attire, and were made for me during many years by the well-known West End firm Samuelson, Linney and Son of . . . Bond Street, London.[47]

A combination of fantasy and authenticity, heightened by Tilley's patronage of Bond Street tailors and her use of a style borrowed from the outrageous dandy the Marquis of Anglesey, lent her risqué characterizations a sense of controlled danger that was immediately marketable despite its perverse associations. Hers was an act that could have succeeded only at a moment of profound transition in the practice and representation of gendered behaviour, grounded in an expansion of the marketplace and a liberalization of sexual mores. The correspondence between Tilley's biological body and the social body she caricatured on stage threw into sharp relief the deep shift in attitudes that some historians have claimed defined the emergence of an anxious state of modernity at the turn of the century, celebrating its more expressive surfaces while hinting at interior crisis.[48]

The man's suit, in all of its supposed solidity, provided a remarkably unstable and thus suitably malleable vessel for such incendiary developments, which continued to smoulder throughout the remainder of the twentieth century. Its paradoxical attractions surfaced once more on the frame of the female body in the 1960s, before postmodernism exploded the sense of a situated identity and rendered the agency of dandyism obsolete. The Algerian-born French designer Yves Saint Laurent sent the ghost of Brummell out into the world for one final promenade. In 1966 he experimented for the first time with the man's formal dinner suit, elongating its line to drape around the curves of the female body, finding in the tension and confusion between boy and girl a new freedom. 'Le Smoking' became a staple in Saint Laurent's repertoire, captured most

Vesta Tilley, music-hall artiste, in 'swell' mode, *c.* 1900.

Helmut Newton, Le Smoking, YSL, rue Aubriot, Paris, 1975.

famously in Helmut Newton's brooding photograph for *Vogue* in September 1975. As Stephen Gundle has observed, the two men – Saint Laurent a gay man born in colonial North Africa, and Newton a refugee from Nazism – were well versed in the fact that

> corruption, authoritarianism and sexual perversion were never far from the centre of the bourgeois subconscious . . . The cultural climate of the seventies allowed them to bring their convictions about the bourgeoisie into the commercial and artistic mainstream.[49]

Sharp tailoring and a fetishistic spin on old-style dandyism provided them with the tools.

Harry Clarke, illustration for Hans Christian Andersen's
'The Emperor's New Clothes', 1916.

FOUR

Seeing the Suit

Many, many years ago there was an emperor who was so
terribly fond of beautiful new clothes that he spent all his
money on his attire. He did not care about his soldiers or
attending the theatre, or even going for a drive in the park,
unless it was to show off his new clothes. He had an outfit
for every hour of the day. And just as we say, 'The king
is in his council chamber', his subjects used to say, 'The
emperor is in his clothes closet.'

Hans Christian Andersen, 'The Emperor's New Clothes'[1]

In April 1837 the Danish storyteller Hans Christian Andersen
published one of his best-loved tales, 'The Emperor's New
Clothes'. Based on a medieval fable from Moorish Spain, in
which fraudulent weavers promise the king a new suit of clothes
that appear invisible to imposters, Andersen's version transformed the basic narrative into an elegant comedy of vanity,
pride, posturing and shame, punctured by the honest innocence
of a child.[2] As the swindled monarch parades naked through
the streets under his crimson canopy, the spectating crowds are
released from their delusion and realize that his magic suit is a
fabrication, a simple confidence trick:

'He has nothing on!' shouted all the people at last. The
emperor shivered, for he was certain that they were

right; but thought, 'I must bear it until the procession is over.' And he walked even more proudly, and the two gentleman of the imperial bedchamber went on carrying the train that wasn't there.[3]

This chapter, following in the emperor's footsteps, traces the suit's enduring fascination as a staple signifier for myriad impulses, not just for writers and folklorists, but also for architects, artists, film-makers and designers. It examines the subtle significance this amalgamation of wool, thread, buckram and underlying flesh has been made to play in a broader history of modern and contemporary cultures. Andersen transposed a century-old tale to the milieu of early nineteenth-century Denmark, and in so doing ensured that the story of the vain emperor in his non-existent suit entered the popular lexicon as an international parable on the foolishness of the gullible. For those with an interest in the psychology of clothing and the sociology of the suit, there is also something in Andersen's elegant economy of words that leads us back to fundamental ideas about the suit's transparency as a symbol for social structures, evolutionary theories and political belief systems.

For example, the *fin-de-siècle* Viennese architect Adolf Loos was, like Andersen, a passionate advocate of the excellent moral and aesthetic properties of true tailoring – and a stern critic of dishonest excess, sartorial or otherwise. More than this, he also proposed a radical theory of architecture and decoration that drew explicit connections between the practice of designing buildings and the framing of clothes around the structure of the body:

The architect's general task is to provide a warm and livable space. Carpets are warm and livable. He decides for this reason to spread out one carpet on the floor and to hang up four to form the four walls.

> But you cannot build a house out of carpets. Both
> the carpet on the floor and the tapestry on the wall
> require a structural frame to hold them in the correct
> place. To invent this frame is the architect's second
> task. This is the correct and logical path to be followed
> in architecture. It was in this sequence that mankind
> learned how to build. In the beginning was dressing.[4]

The simple engineering of the modern suit was a perfect vehicle for an exposition of high modernist architectural principles. Its metaphorical values and symbolism, together with its material characteristics, made it a suitable tool for radical creativity; a lens through which avant-gardism could be focused, not just in the art of building but also, as we shall see, in painting, sculpture, performance, literature, photography, cinema and the practice of fashion itself.

The architectural theorist Mark Wigley uses Loos's obsession with clothing as the basis of an important thesis on the uneasy relationship between fashion and architecture. He shows how Loos's ideas were prefigured by the writings of the mid-nineteenth-century German polymath Gottfried Semper, who first identified 'the textile essence of architecture, the dissimulating fabric, the fabrication of architecture with the clothing of the body.' Semper, Wrigley explained, drew

> on the identity between the German words for wall
> (Wand) and dress (Gewand) to establish the 'Principle
> of Dressing' as the 'true essence' of architecture . . .
> But [he also established that] architecture does not
> follow or resemble clothing. On the contrary, clothing
> follows architecture.[5]

There is something in this hierarchical positioning that reveals the egoism of the architect and his (for it is almost always a he) compromised attachment to sartorial appearances. In portrait photographs and satirical cartoons it is no coincidence that master architects always appear so concerned with the appropriate presentation of the self. If the suit ever gained a reputation for pompous stuffiness or refined pretension it was surely helped by the architect's propensity to translate architectural theory through the content of his wardrobe. Paired with heavily rimmed spectacles and a bow tie, accessorized with crisp white shirt (sometimes without a collar), tailored sharply in dark grey Melton to mimic the technocrat, retrospectively in the thick hairy tweed of the professor or country squire, democratically in workman's baggy blue serge or futuristically in Japanese synthetics, the suits of Adolf Loos, Le Corbusier, Ludwig Mies van der Rohe, Frank Lloyd Wright, Basil Spence, Philip Johnson, Richard Rogers, Norman Foster, Rem Koolhaas and many others have been created to be as worthy of celebration as their buildings, and have often been as carefully planned and executed.

Part of the reason for this sartorial obsession lay in the revulsion first-wave architectural modernists felt towards decorative feminized ornament and their translation of this into a series of professional diktats. If women's love of fashionable clothing shared in a 'primitive' fascination for bright, ephemeral and intricate surfaces, then men's suits provided a rational and ordered metaphor for stability and civilization. Le Corbusier set the rules down explicitly in his essay 'Towards a New Architecture' of 1923:

> Decoration is of a sensorial and elementary order; as is colour, and is suited to simple races, peasants and savages . . . The peasant loves ornament and decorates his walls. The civilized man wears a well-cut suit and is the owner of easel pictures and books. Decoration is the essential surplus, the quantum of the peasant; and

Le Corbusier in the fashionable double-breasted suit of the mid-twentieth century, worn with characteristic panache.

Sir Basil Spence, architect of some of Britain's most significant modernist
buildings, combines Edwardian tweeds and whiskers with the 1960s paisley tie.

proportion is the essential surplus, the quantum of the cultivated man.[6]

Another factor in the glorification of tailoring by modernists was the ability of the suit to adapt to and reflect the circumstances and characteristics of modern life. In his subsequent treatise *The Decorative Art of Today* of 1925, Le Corbusier set out five new approaches to design that were necessary for the overhaul of the environment and society in modernity. All paid direct or indirect homage to the properties of contemporary menswear. Utilitarianism was the first of these:

> Utilitarian need calls for tools, brought in every respect
> to that degree of perfection seen in industry. This
> then is the great programme for the decorative arts.
> Day after day industry is turning out tools of perfect
> utility and convenience that soothe our spirits with the
> luxury afforded by the elegance of their conception,
> the purity of their execution, and the efficiency of
> their operation. This rational perfection and this
> precise formulation constitute sufficient ground
> between them to allow the recognition of a style.[7]

The idea of clothing as tool had of course been one of the underpinning concepts that smoothed the rise of the English gentleman's wardrobe as a paradigm of civilized taste in the early nineteenth century. The hard-wearing textiles and functional patterns associated with dressing for the country estate, the Empire and the parade ground found an easy translation into the style and repertoire of tailoring associated with Savile Row and adapted for the boardroom and banking hall of the modern metropolis. Advances in fastenings, ease of pressing and waterproofing, all slickly promoted in contemporary advertising rhetoric, presented the suit as the prototypical machine for

living in, long before the invention of the suntrap balcony and single-pane window.

Vladimir Lenin at his Kremlin desk, 1918.

To celebrate elegant appearances for their own sake ran the risk of inviting ridicule for effeminacy or, worse, homosexuality, but when sartorial form could be discussed in terms of its resistance to wear or weather, or the perfection of its construction, then the right of its owner to accrue a reputation for his impeccable style remained unquestioned. Yet the taint of aristocratic taste also imbued the modern suit with the problematic patina of old-fashioned elitism. Le Corbusier was compelled to look to a more self-consciously classless role model, whose political style chimed with the demotic appeal of the mass-produced as effortlessly as the old-style milord pulled on his tweeds:

Lenin is seated at the Rotonde on a cane chair; he has
paid twenty centimes for his coffee with a tip of one sou.
He has drunk out of a small, white porcelain cup. He is
wearing a bowler hat and a smooth white collar. He has
been writing for several hours on sheets of typing paper.
His inkpot is smooth and round, made from bottle glass.
He is learning to govern one hundred million people.[8]

Similarly, if the genealogy of the gentleman's suit lay in
the leisured pursuits of the aristocracy, any claim about its
democratic potential was fraught with difficulty. Thus from
Lenin's embodiment of a banal yet revolutionary modernity, Le
Corbusier extended his celebration of utility to an account of
the role of the functional object (which included the suit) in
freeing the user from older notions of service and social hierarchy. In the third of his propositions, the adaptability of the
industrial product (the simple, expendable lounge suit) is com-
mended as a metaphor for a utopian vision of social equality:

The objects of utility in our lives have freed the slaves of
a former age. They are in fact themselves slaves, menials,
servants. Do you want them as your soul mates? We sit
on them, work on them, use them up; when used up we
replace them. We demand from such servants precision
and care, decency and an unassertive presence.[9]

Once again, it is possible to read a surviving version of
classic dandyism between the lines: the justification for sartorial
consumption wrapped up in a reverence for the perfected and
unfettered performance. In the late eighteenth century patriotic
pamphleteers and caricaturists had often contrasted the well-
clothed, healthy form of John Bull with the ragged, emaciated
frame of the French peasant. The belligerent freeborn Englishman sported the products of early mass production as trophies

of his superiority. Similarly, those French painters and writers enamoured of equality, fraternity and liberty frequently chose the deceptively simple garb of the English gentry as costume for their revolutionary thinkers. Plain speaking, plain living and utterly efficient, the old self-deluded modernist morphed effortlessly into the new. Le Corbusier's twentieth-century John Bull used the democratizing promises of the modern wardrobe as an excuse to consume. Metal zip fasteners and seams secured by sewing machines had replaced the nostalgic notion of the bespoke, but the cheaper suits that resulted offered all comers the promise of functional and elegant clothing. As with fashion, so with the accessible modern luxury of the cruise liner, the apartment block and the motor car.

If, by the 1920s, political reform and internationalism were causing the spectre of class strife and the ideal of the nation state to seem momentarily outdated as philosophical motors for the revolutionary justification or condemnation of the pleasures of fashionable consumption, a deeper-rooted misogyny held out as a refuge from which the architect-dandy could play fashion against function and still emerge with suit unsullied. Le Corbusier certainly made full use of the contrast between plain, wholesome 'masculine' objects and decorative, debased 'feminine' ones in his push for a standard of taste that combined the best characteristics of the mass-produced and the bespoke in its quest for modern beauty:

> Trash is always abundantly decorated; the luxury object
> is well-made, neat and clean, pure and healthy, and in
> its bareness reveals the quality of its manufacture . . .
> Surface elaboration, if extended over everything,
> becomes repugnant and scandalous.[10]

And in *The Decorative Art of Today* he drew on the rhetoric of the healthy body and the corrupting effect of sexual desire

You be D__m'd

Vous etes une Bete

Pub.^d by H Humphrey St James Street

With Porter Roast Beef & Plumb Pudding well cram'd.
Jack English declares that Monsr may be D__d *POLITENESS,*
The Soup Meagre Frenchman such Language dont suit,
So he Grins Indignation & calls him a Brute.

The honest manners and attire of John Bull are contrasted with the effete affectation of the Frenchman in this satirical print of the late 1770s.

to heighten his sense of terror at the threat posed to a rational universe by the excesses of feminine culture.

A stress on hygiene thus joined utility, a celebration of contemporary modernity, democratization and a rejection of useless decoration on the architect's agenda for the reformation of popular taste and the built environment. The modern man's suit was clearly the most appropriate uniform for the task in hand. The underlying codes for building a new world found their origins not just in the promises of Fordism or the hard technology of the industrial workshop, but in a more established set of Platonic rules and practices engineered for the social, economic and ethical behaviour of the triumphant 'clothes-wearing man'.

To return to the ideas of Loos, whose most influential essay, 'Ornament and Crime', Le Corbusier had reprinted in the first

"J'AI FAILLI ATTENDRE"

COSTUME VESTON, DE LUS ET BEFVE

Fashion plate, *Gazette du Bon Ton*, 1922.

issue of his journal *L'Esprit nouveau* in 1920, this fundamental concept – that male clothing had reached an evolutionary state of standardization and convenience that placed it on a more rational plane than the cyclical, corrupting and sexually driven dress of women – was central to the twentieth century's understanding of itself, 'a mark behind which the individual is shielded from the increasingly threatening and seemingly uncontrollable forces of modern life (forces that were themselves understood as feminine)'.[11] Like modern architecture itself, the male wardrobe was designed to act as a physical and psychological buffer against the confusing sensations of modernity. In this liminal status, between interior/body and exterior/world, the suit was an obvious canvas for the imaginings of the avant-garde.[12]

Nowhere were those imaginings so extreme as in the projections of the Italian Futurists, who in the first three decades of the twentieth century elected not to reify the suit's classicism, as architectural modernists had done, but to tear it apart in a passionate outburst of artistic iconoclasm. As the art historian Radu Stern has demonstrated, the essence of Futurist thinking on clothing lay in an anti-fashion impulse and a desire to inculcate a new aesthetics based on a kinetic understanding of an ephemeral modernity. The artist Giacomo Balla was the pioneer in this respect, both setting out a number of manifestos for the reform of contemporary dress, and designing and making his own wardrobe in response to those ideas. The man's suit was the material through which he set about rupturing conventional attitudes to clothing. His manifesto *Male Futurist Dress*, published in May 1914, challenged the dull tones, symmetry and uniformity that characterized conventional apparel (particularly at a moment when Europe was militarizing and moving towards war) with a more dynamic approach to dressing achieved through sporting metaphors, an avant-garde approach to pattern-cutting and a sensual embrace of colour, texture and even scent.[13] In eleven pithy statements, Balla promised a wardrobe that would

IL VESTITO ANTINEUTRALE

Manifesto futurista

Glorifichiamo la guerra,
sola igiene del mondo.
MARINETTI.
(1° Manifesto del Futurismo - 20 Febbraio 1909)

Viva Asinari di Bernezzo!
MARINETTI.
(1ª Serata futurista - Teatro Lirico, Milano, Febbraio 1910)

L'umanità si vestì sempre di **quiete,** di **paura,** di **cautela** o d'**indecisione,** portò sempre il lutto, o il piviale, o il mantello. Il corpo dell'uomo fu sempre diminuito da sfumature e da tinte **neutre,** avvilito dal nero, soffocato da cinture, imprigionato da panneggiamenti.

Fino ad oggi gli uomini usarono abiti di colori e forme statiche, cioè drappeggiati, solenni, gravi, incomodi e sacerdotali. Erano espressioni di timidezza, di malinconia e di **schiavitù,** negazione della vita muscolare, che soffocava in un passatismo anti-igienico di stoffe troppo pesanti e di mezze tinte tediose, effeminate o decadenti. Tonalità e ritmi di **pace desolante,** funeraria e deprimente.

OGGI vogliamo abolire:

1. — Tutte le tinte **neutre,** « carine », sbiadite, *fantasia,* semioscure e umilianti.

2. — Tutte le tinte e le foggie pedanti, professorali e teutoniche. I disegni a righe, a quadretti, a **puntini diplomatici.**

3. — I vestiti da lutto, nemmeno adatti per i becchini. Le morti eroiche non devono essere compiante, ma ricordate con vestiti rossi.

4. — L'equilibrio **mediocrista,** il cosidetto buon gusto e la cosidetta armonia di tinte e di forme, che frenano gli entusiasmi e rallentano il passo.

5. — La simmetria nel taglio, le linee **statiche,** che stancano, deprimono, contristano, legano i muscoli; l'uniformità di goffi risvolti e tutte le cincischiature. I bottoni inutili. I colletti e i polsini inamidati.

Noi futuristi vogliamo liberare la nostra razza da ogni **neutralità,** dall'indecisione paurosa e quietista, dal pessimismo negatore e dall'inerzia

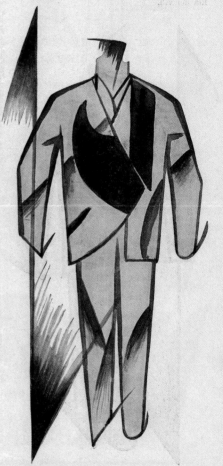

Vestito bianco - rosso - verde
del parolibero futurista Marinetti. *(Mattino)*

Giacomo Balla, 'The Anti-Neutral Suit', *Futurist Manifesto*, May 1914.

'liberate humanity from slow Romantic nostalgia and the difficulty of life'. Its prismatic tones would transform the city in a maelstrom of 'three dimensional colour acrobatics, which will generate innumerable new abstractions of dynamic rhythms in the growing futurist sensibility'.[14]

If Balla provided an anti-suit theory, the artist-designer Ernesto Michahelles, who worked under the name Thayaht, produced the product. His revolutionary tuta (or TuTa, a utilitarian adaption of the worker's overall, which aimed to make the oppressive concept of fashion for women redundant) and his collaborations with the French couturier Madeleine Vionnet brought him some notoriety among the Florentine intelligentsia. But it was his own *Manifesto for the Transformation of Male Clothing*, written with his brother Ruggero in 1932, that really lent practical weight to Balla's earlier imaginings. Thayaht was emphatic in his rejection of conformity:

> We have to abolish the black-and-white typographic cliché of the evening dress and of all puritan and Anglo-Saxon, northern and anti-Mediterranean cuts. We thus have to eliminate collars, cuffs, belts, adjustable loops, suspenders, garters, and all symbols of slavery that hinder blood circulation and freedom of movement (the often-ignored causes of lack of appetite, feelings of faintness, bad temper, and family quarrels or friction). We have to eliminate linings, useless pockets and irrational rows of buttons, trouser cuffs, berets, petticoats, half belts, collars, padding, and other similar antique, ridiculous, and anti-sporting remnants that are nothing other than dirt and sweat collectors.[15]

The synthetic clothing that was designed to replace these garments aspired to a practical and aesthetic perfection that would,

Thayaht claimed, transform the fashion industry and its wearers' quality of life. Sixteen distinct modular pieces, from a multi-functional undershirt to a hat incorporating radio receivers, provided the basics of a post-suit wardrobe that blended science-fiction fantasy with Arts and Crafts whimsy. Thayaht was not alone in his proselytizing. In England, the home of sartorial conformity, the Men's Dress Reform Party (founded in 1929) echoed the Futurists' call. Its round of lectures, contests, letters to newspapers and publicity stunts drew attention to a cause that simply wished for comfort and expression in men's clothing. Eccentric though it may have seemed, the party's aims in fact anticipated many of the hygienic improvements and social advances that would see true transformation in the quality and choice of ordinary men's dress by the 1950s; and along with rambling, vegetarianism and sun-worship, its simple anti-Victorian creed drew significant followers, with almost two hundred branches across North America and Europe and a shop selling its advanced wares on the French Riviera by the end of the 1930s.[16] Artistic and intellectual posturing clearly carried cultural clout.

The suit's essential yet misleading conformism was interesting to a wide range of artists beyond the more progressive fringes of architecture and design. Its intrinsically 'modern' qualities, both positive and negative, drew attention as much for the metaphorical possibilities its form suggested, as for the desire to inculcate wholesale reform in the material and visual world of things. The first inklings of this enduring fascination coincided with the rise of Impressionist painting, and were captured in the associated flowering in France of literary and journalistic works of the 1860s and '70s whose focus was the relationship between fashion and modernity. In Paris, in particular, the idea of fashion was adopted as a code through which the wider changes inflicted on society by the forces of modernity could be interpreted and critiqued. To understand

Thayat, the TuTa, 1919.

the details of fashion's development and be interested in their wider implications was a sign of the artist's engagement with the challenge of modern life itself and an indication of his status as a member of the avant-garde.[17]

Baudelaire, Gautier, Balzac, Mallarmé, Zola and, later, Proust all engaged with modern fashion as one of the great preoccupations of the age. And while their attention was largely focused on the problem and allure of the fashionable woman – literally fashioning a symbolist language of impressions derived from the shimmering effects of the contemporary feminine wardrobe – the foil against which such beauty glimmered was inevitably composed of masculine things. Fashionable men were indeed the key producers, writers, painters, readers and viewers of the beau monde, and their inconspicuous dark suits were an essential element of the *mise en scène*. The critic Edmond Duranty, champion of Degas and author of 'The New Painting' (1876), could see how their translation into paint provided a sharpened sense of the present, more prescient even than the rapid whirl of women's dress. A generation of artists including Manet, Renoir, Bazille, Caillebotte, Whistler, Tissot, Sargent and even Cézanne appeared to follow Duranty's advice:

What we need is that special note of the modern individual, in his clothes, in the middle of his social routines, at home or in the street. The data becomes singularly penetrating: this is fitting the pencil with a flaming torch, it's the study of moral reflections on physiognomies and clothing, the observation of man in the privacy of his apartment, of that special trait stamped on him by his profession, the gestures it causes him to make, cross sections of the aspects of his life that allow him to grow best and cause him to stand out most. With a back we want a temperament to be revealed, an age, a social state; with a pair of hands,

Pierre-Auguste Renoir, *Eugène Murer* in contemporary dress, 1877, oil on canvas. Murer was a fellow artist, chef, poet and art collector; a connoisseur, like Renoir and other Impressionists, of the sensations of modern life.

Gilbert and George pose in their studio in Spitalfields, London, 2005.

we must express a judge or a merchant; by a gesture,
a whole string of feelings . . . The way he carries
himself will teach us that this person is going to
a business meeting, and that other is returning from
a tryst.[18]

The suit's continuing function as a memorandum both
for modernity's predictable routines and for its darker, irra-
tional hinterlands is evident in its recurring appearance as a
prop for avant-garde art movements from Dada and Surrealism
(most pointedly in Duchamp's cross-gendered masquerades and
Magritte's suburban dream worlds), through to the performed
conceptualism of Beuys and of the London-based performance
artists Gilbert and George (where felt and tweed come to represent the material power of the subconscious, to operate as
fetishes of memory). Gilbert and George, in particular, put the
seeming normality of the tailored suit (made for them by a local
tailor in the then less-than-glamorous environs of Shoreditch)
at the centre of their mannered self-presentation. Here they drily
outline its nostalgic and quotidian attractions in an interview
with the contemporary art curator Hans Ulrich Obrist of 1995:

> *How did the suits come about?*
> GILBERT: George always had suits, so did I – not maybe
>   when I was working – but otherwise suits.
> GEORGE: Because we come from the country. In the
>   '50s, on any important occasion – if you went to
>   church, or someone got married, if you went on
>   holiday – you had to put on a suit.
> GILBERT: George always used to have a black suit he
>   always wore at art school. He was a dandy a little,
>   already in '65. In the beginning when we didn't
>   have money they were second hand suits.
> GEORGE: We had our Burton suits in '72 probably.

Why three buttons?

GILBERT: We like them.

GEORGE: It's normal. We always think that if you took a suit from every decade this century and made an average, you'd probably end up like this – they're not particularly 1990's, not particularly 1950's.

But why do up all three buttons?

GEORGE: That's to be tidy I think. Tailors always tell you to leave the bottom one undone, they even tailor it like that now. We have to change the cut to do up all three buttons. When I was a teenager, the family always told you to leave the bottom one undone . . .

GILBERT: But it's become so everybody copies our suits. What's exciting is that we have all these photographs of artists from 1971, 2, 3, 4 – at parties, all drunk. And we always looked the same. The others looked like hippies, with beards, flared jackets. Everybody has suits now – the young artists, the pop stars.[19]

Gilbert and George use the suit as a subtle means of amplifying those 'abnormal' tendencies that linger beneath the apparently placid surfaces of certain aspects of English culture (in the freak show and the waxwork chamber of horrors). Their stiffly buttoned-up two-pieces bespeak the unspeakable closet racism, homosocial queerness and parochial patriotism that resurface in their photographic and performance works. Such polite but unnerving respectability inevitably hides scatological intent.

Other artists have employed more overt visual strategies to describe and contest a history of difference. The practices of black dandyism have provided rich terrain for the renegotiation 'of oppressive ideologies and degrading images of blackness'.[20]

Iké Udé, *Sartorial Anarchy 30*, 2013, pigment on satin paper.

In the fields of film-making, photography and performance, a generation coming to maturity in the 1980s and '90s drew on a longer heritage of deliberated suit-wearing to hone what some have termed a post-black aesthetic. Stretching from London to New York and delineating a new post-colonial Black Atlantic, the vivid talents of artists including Isaac Julien, Iké Udé and Yinka Shonibare have recrafted the sartorial terrain in a series of devastating critiques of the suit's place in a political and economic history of sexual and racial repression: Julien, with his poetic reimagining of the forbidden desires of the Harlem Renaissance poet Langston Hughes; Udé with his reconceptualization of dandified technique in a context of hyper-branded consumerism; and Shonibare in his restaging of High Victorian imperialism in West African fabric. All three evoke the cultural critic Stuart Hall's highlighting of the embodied nature of black style: the very suited-ness of a deeply sartorial turn in black cultural production:

> I ask you to note how, within the black repertoire, style
> – which mainstream cultural critics often believe to be
> the mere husk, the wrapping, the sugar coating on the
> pill – has become itself the subject of what is going on
> . . . think of how these cultures have used the body –
> as if it was, and often it was, the only cultural capital
> we had. We have worked on ourselves as the canvases
> of representation.[21]

Hall's strategy was not confined to black culture; the suit as a focus for work on power, identity and embodiment was a core feature of mainstream postmodern cultural production as well. In the slippages between art, music and video the characteristically broad-shouldered silhouette of 1980s business attire made a regular appearance. In 1984 the American art-pop band Talking Heads released the concert film *Stop Making Sense* with director Jonathan Demme, in which the lead singer, David Byrne, famously wore an ever-expanding grey suit for the song 'Girlfriend Is Better'. Closer to the stylized gestures of Noh theatre or the gallery installations of Beuys than to standard rock stage garb, the costume was a clever satire on contemporary posturing (this was the era of the thrusting yuppie) and the monstrous artist's ego. Two years later, in 1986, the British band New Order also looked to art and the suit as inspiration, for the video to their song 'Bizarre Love Triangle'. The New York artist and film-maker Robert Longo directed and provided the imagery, drawing on his life-sized drawings of thrashing be-suited men to create haunting sequences of falling figures, eerily predictive of the footage of victims plunging from the windows of the World Trade Center's twin towers in September 2001.[22]

Beyond its mobilization as a vehicle for postmodern art and music, directors and costume designers for popular film, alongside cinema critics and theorists, have also well understood the use of the suit as a canvas for representation. Some of the most iconic films of the twentieth century have at their core a leading actor whose wardrobe functions as a central prop for either characterization or narrative drive. In Alfred Hitchcock's classic *North by Northwest*, released in 1959, the Madison Avenue executive Roger Thornhill (played by Cary Grant) is mistaken for a government spy and chased by shadowy double agents through a series of complex Cold War scenarios while seemingly maintaining his sartorial cool in a characteristically elegant costume. Grant's suit in its iconic indestructability functions both as a religious cipher and as art. In an echo of the Holy Trinity it represents simultaneously our common understanding of the spirit of the classic suit in its unchanging everyday sense; the suit as a medium for the screenplay's incredible narrative twists and turns; and the suit as it reflects and constructs the reassuringly dapper appearance of the film's star.[23]

David Byrne, promotion for *Stop Making Sense* (1984).

Cary Grant (centre) in Alfred Hitchcock's *North by Northwest* (1959).

Jonathan Faiers, in his recent analysis of the unsettling role played by fashion in film, spends some time discussing Cary Grant's wardrobe in *North by Northwest* and other notable films including *Charade* and *Bringing Up Baby*. Acknowledging Grant's status as one of the most debonair of Hollywood's stars – known for his immaculate elegance on and off screen, aided by his patronage of the Savile Row tailor Kilgour, French & Stanbury and his exquisite physique and manners – Faiers bestows a particular magic upon Grant's suits, which still, half a century later, retain the power of amulets:

> The majority of suits on screen function fairly simply,
> connoting respectability, authority and conservatism,

193

but there are certain sets of clothing that transcend
this expected function and assume a super-functional
existence as 'armour-plated' suits which bestow a
mythical status on their wearers.[24]

Grant's suits were not the only magical suits in Tinseltown,
however. The white suit developed and worn by Alec Guinness's
character Sidney Stratton in the Ealing satire *The Man in the
White Suit* of 1951 shared in the paranoid obsessions of the
1950s. The suit's revolutionary qualities (its surfaces promise
to resist dirt and decay) threaten to destabilize workers' secur-
ity in the British textile industry, and the film operates as a
metaphor for the threat of both communism and unconstrained
capitalism (favouring in its outcome a very British sense of
muddle and compromise). As did those of Andersen's emperor,
Stratton's new clothes isolate him as a figure of ridicule: 'His
white suit changes from being the symbol of intellectual and
scientific brilliance to that of a livery of shame, marking [him]
out as an enemy of the people . . . whose dazzling appearance
offers him no chance of escape.'[25] More topically, in its startling
brightness and modishly ample cut Stratton's suit replays some
of the moral debates about fashion and the body that had very
recently concerned critics of Dior's glamorous New Look for
women.[26] In the hands of directors as accomplished as Hitchcock
or Alexander Mackendrick, post-war tailoring could clearly be
transformed into potent storytelling material.

Of even greater influence as symbolic and socially affective
props are those suits taken up by the fictional character James
Bond in the adaptations of Ian Fleming's spy novels that began
in 1962 with Terence Young's *Dr No*, starring Sean Connery.
Working-class, Edinburgh-born Connery, while less refined in
demeanour than Fleming's literary hero, brought to the role
an 'everyman' appeal that echoed the opening out of the rules
and regulations of sexuality and class that were concurrently

Poster for Ealing Studios' *The Man in the White Suit* (1951).

Sean Connery as James Bond in *Dr No* (1962).

redefining the bodies and suits of young British men. Andrew Spicer summarizes the key to Connery's success very well:

> He incarnated both the unwavering patriotism of the traditional British gentleman hero and the guiltless sexual philandering of the international playboy who embodied the Swinging Sixties. Bond became, on both sides of the Atlantic, a hero of consumption, refined, hedonistic and liberated . . . He was both a guy like them and the projection of audiences' aspirational fantasy of stylish and successful living, the classless hero of a modern, expansive international meritocracy. One of the reviewers for *Dr No* praised Connery as 'a flawless choice for the snob hero, Bond; virile, tough, perfectly tailored and faultlessly knowing.'[27]

In a sense, despite the apparent deficiencies in his personal background, Connery's reticent machismo offered the ideal mannequin around which Fleming's discreet indications of flawless style could be dressed. Resisting the flamboyance of fashion, Connery's elegant suits, fitted by the tailor Anthony Sinclair of Conduit Street, adhered to the pared-down rules of the guardsman, and changed little over the course of the six Bond films in which he appeared before 1971.[28]

Later screen Bonds appeared in costumes that were much more closely aligned to fads. Roger Moore's safari suits, flared trousers and widening lapels were nevertheless vital signifiers of the loucher context of the 1970s and early '8os, carefully modulated to within an inch of parody by the society tailor and Swinging London stalwart Doug Hayward. From the film *GoldenEye* in 1995 to *Casino Royale* in 2006, Pierce Brosnan and Daniel Craig found their more active bodies described through the smoother lines of the Roman tailor Brioni, reflecting both the dominance of Italian taste in menswear during the period and the industrial efficiency of the firm (favoured by the costume designer Lindy Hemming). The American designer Tom Ford, who was also indebted to Italian tailoring tradition, continued the sharper, international theme in Craig's subsequent roles.[29] As we move further forward in time from the original settings of Fleming's novels, perhaps it is inevitable that those indications of a circumspect and tightly controlled version of British masculinity that were sewn into Connery's suits should have unravelled a little. But it seems clear that the suit's role as vessel for aspirational promise, albeit in terms of a truly global audience, continues as an unchallenged facet of the Bond franchise.

In a world where novelty is prized and the dissolving of unchanging Bond-like values often goes un-mourned (except by vintage-obsessed nostalgics), how are we to assess the status of the suit itself? Beyond simple aesthetic, literary or cinematic

Daniel Craig as James Bond in *Skyfall* (2012).

forms of representation, and in a design context where narrative meaning has become an integral part of the marketing and understanding of fashion, how has the material suit become its own cipher? In the twenty-first century the language of tailoring persists as part of the altered lexicon of avant-garde fashion, often blurring with the interests of contemporary art practice; so we can be sure that whatever physical form it takes, the new language of the suit will remain a complex and challenging one. But the pressing question persists: if we could see the emperor's new clothes, what would they look like?

In many ways, what we might call 'the new suit' is a phenomenon of the revised position of fashion in modernity more generally (its radicalization). Where once the cultural and economic function of high fashion was either to foment social and aesthetic change from a position of influence, or (in the case of the middle market) to respond to such change in a wider industrial context, now the self-defined role of radical fashion seems to be to present a very specialized commentary on the vicissitudes of contemporary existence. This is often an insular critique that bears little relationship to the immediate concerns of mainstream clothing manufacturers and consumers, but has everything to do with internal cultural debates on genre, hierarchy, presentation and style, and more pragmatically with capturing the right sort of attention. In this sense the natural home of the directional fashion statement (for menswear as much as womenswear) now resides in the art and design museum, the specialized website, the scholarly journal, the glossy monograph and the niche magazine, rather than in the street, the shop or the wardrobe. In their detail, such products often seem destined to be showcased rather than sold for wear, and their strikingly remote but often painfully beautiful manifestations are artefactual in the purest sense, embodying a level of craft and a discursive power that lie beyond market concerns or functional facility.

In his Autumn/Winter 2009 show, 'The McQueensbury Rules', in Milan, Alexander McQueen displayed his flair for elegant subversion, producing a menacing interpretation of *fin-de-siècle* dandyism.

Indeed, the protagonists in this field (including Rei Kawakubo, Vivienne Westwood, Alexander McQueen, Dries Van
Noten, Martin Margiela and Hedi Slimane and others more
closely allied to the traditional tailoring trades, including Richard
James and Thom Browne) have regularly stressed their affinity
with the working practices of architects, artists, musicians and
philosophers, deliberately eschewing any reference to commerce
in discussions of their work. Of his generation, Alexander
McQueen was perhaps the most talented interpreter of the suit's
inherent beauty. Cut with a confidence and passion that transformed the body and evoked endless associations with history
and the world of ideas, his suits for men and women pushed at
the very boundaries of possibility and evoke a sense of longing
that is beyond normal satisfaction. Interviewed by Susannah
Frankel for *AnOther Man* magazine in 2006, McQueen almost
seemed to acknowledge the suit's intangibility, its infinite play
with meaning, himself:

> Tailoring is just a form of construction, it's the rigour
> behind the design but at the end of the day you're still
> dealing with a single or double-breasted jacket. The
> narrative is what makes it interesting, plus the romance
> behind it and the detail . . . That's what makes McQueen
> stand out, the detail. I want the clothes to be heirlooms,
> like they used to be . . . In the end, when you go back to
> something, it's about how you've moved on. For me, it's
> all about the fact that I'm capable of doing anything as
> long as it comes from the heart.[30]

Unsurprisingly, some critics have viewed such opinions,
indeed the very notion of radical fashion, as effete nonsense,
a symptom of crippling intellectual and moral decadence. Yet
such haunting imagery, particularly when derived from the
Platonic forms of the tailored suit, provides an apt conclusion

to the progress of an object-type whose form has provided a unique focus for debate, dissent and degeneration over the course of its four-hundred-year evolution, and whose twenty-first-century shadows represent a gradual atrophying of its former power as a medium of social change and control.[31]

EPILOGUE:
Future Suits

In an article in the *London Review of Books* in 2014, the Scottish novelist Andrew O'Hagan mused on the state of men's dress after visiting the menswear shows at London Fashion Week. His approach was tart and satirical, remarking – as have so many observers before him – on the enduring nonsense that constitutes high fashion. Tracing the 'peacock' tendency back to the immature interests of King Edward VII and noting a continuing concern with frippery among those 'pedants of the knicker' (fashion journalists, photographers, stylists, bloggers, designers and groupies) who had flocked to the London shows, O'Hagan marvelled at the customs of an obscure tribe. Like a nineteenth-century explorer or anthropologist, he both extolled its arcane exoticism and identified a renewed vibrancy in a close-knit culture that seemed far from extinct:

> There were something like seventy shows in over three days, some of them glitzy to the point of blindness and others, well, a bit worked up. Being worked up is the natural state of the person overly interested in cool . . . The Richard James show, held in a long glass corridor on Park Lane . . . had a military theme, depicting the savoir-faire of the Desert Rats, their khaki humility, their blond and fawn reserve, as opposed to their real-life fear and thirst on the baking sand. In the new dispensation, prints of colonial maps make their way

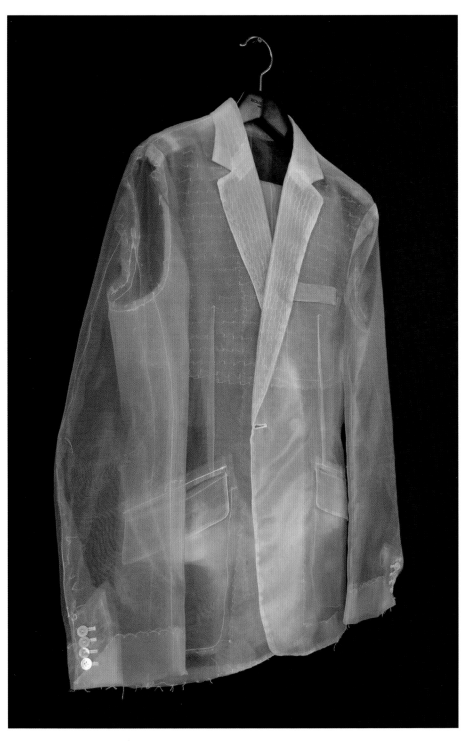

The Naked Suit, by Richard James in collaboration with artist Spencer
Tunick for *Esquire* magazine in 2009.

on to shirts, while crisp white suits come emblazoned
with flowers from an imaginary oasis.[1]

O'Hagan was translating a very real contemporary phenomenon for the rarefied readership of the LRB, but its effects
have been apparent in the mass media for several years. British
sociologists had spent much of the late 1980s and '90s analysing
it, focusing on an apparent crisis in traditional concepts of
masculinity that had produced a fresh category in the history
of consumption: the new man and his fashionable equivalent,
the metrosexual.[2] Echoing these shifts in consumer identity,
menswear designers have also been enjoying a much wider profile in the past two decades, and the language in which concepts
and new lines are now promoted has come to share common
ground with the hyperbolic discourse generally associated with
high-end womenswear. This renaissance in menswear clearly
reflects the changing economic and social context in which
men's clothing is designed, sold and consumed. As the fashion
theorist José Teunissen has argued, the financial crisis, environ-
mental concerns and a generation of consumers attuned to
quality have created a space in which a more nuanced version
of male sartorialism has thrived: global luxury brands have
been able to direct niche, high-performance products to a discerning male market while sales to women have stagnated.
Promotions orientated to a new aspirational middle class in
India and China have further strengthened, rather than dam-
aged, the producers of bespoke and luxury goods. Meanwhile
the objectification of the ideal male body, honed through sport
and enhanced by cosmetics, has redirected the gaze of the nar-
cissistic new man towards himself. In all these developments,
the long-standing values of perfect form and function attached
to menswear have endured, even prospered.[3]

Behind all this marketing hype, the suit itself has remained a
vessel for creativity and a thing of beauty. More open to the

incursions of avant-gardism than ever, its classic lines have proved irresistible to recent generations of menswear designers keen to prove their iconoclastic intent. In 2008 the fashion journalist Hywel Davies followed the trend and produced a compendium of established and emerging talent in Europe and the United States that provided beguiling visual evidence for the Royal College of Art menswear tutor Ike Rust's assertion that 'what has actually happened is that womenswear is now so dull that it is creatively eclipsed by menswear.'[4] In fashion it is a truism to say that there is nothing new under the sun, and it is interesting to draw parallels with that earlier peacock revolution in London's Carnaby Street and King's Road, during which another Royal College of Art tutor produced a book and predicted great things for the future of men's fashion.[5] But where the revolution of the 1960s remained local and rapidly burned itself out, the appetite for new and inspiring variations of sartorialism in 2016 appears to be more enduring and to have a far wider reach.

Claudio Del Vecchio, CEO of Brooks Brothers, in their Regent Street Store, 2008.

Ozwald Boateng, 2007.

Paul Smith at the Oxford Union debate, 1997.

Paul Smith, men's collection, Autumn/Winter 2008–9.

In the style of those listicles that currently seem to constitute what is left of mainstream arts journalism, it is tempting to namecheck the fifteen most significant menswear designers of the twenty-first century whose work has guaranteed a future for the suit as a meaningful modern object. Of the more established British generation Paul Smith and Vivienne Westwood, in their very different idioms, have ensured that the grammar of Mod and Punk continues to inform the language of the suit. Their ebullient eclecticism finds particular favour in international, particularly Asian, markets. Ozwald Boateng and Richard James have performed a similar feat in modernizing the stuffy rhetoric of Savile Row with vivid colour and a sharper cut. In Antwerp, Dries Van Noten and Martin Margiela introduced respectively a refocusing on craft and high-quality material and a rigorous conceptualism. They were echoing, arguably, the existing practices of Japanese designers Yohji Yamamoto and Rei Kawakubo. In the luxury business, Tom Ford and Christopher Bailey deserve credit for their reprioritization of directional menswear in the portfolios of Gucci and Burberry respectively. And for deliberate provocation and incendiary skill, Alexander McQueen, Hedi Slimane, Bernhard Willhelm, Thom Browne and Raf Simons have all introduced an unprecedented level of sublimity or eye-catching absurdism into the repertoire of the suit.

Stylistic and aesthetic advances have been enhanced by technological innovation. As an evolving form of technology in its own right, the suit has offered a very appropriate canvas for the recent discoveries of those in the fashion and textile industries who have become neophiles, championing future possibilities. In the current marketplace, suits made to measure through the precision of body-scanning and produced by means of digital printing, engineered to resist staining and creasing or to preclude the need for expensive dry-cleaning, are either familiar items on the shop rail or at prototype stage, ready for mass dissemination. In the realms of science fiction and avant-garde experimentation,

Female menswear model Elliott Sailors walks the catwalk at Vivienne Westwood's men's collection, Autumn/ Winter 2015.

the language of the suit has lent itself to pioneering investigations of clothing as a weapon against violent attack or surveillance and a communications device in the transmission of big data; an ecological framework for the growing of new bio-textiles; and a membrane for medical and psychological intervention, administering drugs to the body or enhancing mood.[6] Its timeless adaptability has ensured the suit's survival as an icon and medium of modernity.

And in the more mundane circumstances of everyday life, my younger friends in the law and the City assure me that, despite the efforts of those advocates of dress-down Friday or digital-era informality, the suit remains a prized symbol of distinction and power in the professions. Across the United States the reassuring formality of Brooks Brothers continues to inform office etiquette. In academic and art circles, although I find myself reverting to the tweeds, jeans and brogues of a sad middle-aged hipsterdom for most occasions, ceremonial and formal duties do find me reaching regularly for the charcoal lounge suit and the black-tie ensemble. Broadly speaking, my wardrobe habits have not evolved far from those that would have dictated the appearance of my father's or grandfather's generation. In all this there is reason to hold out hope that the suit will endure for another four hundred years, provided those values of reason, equality, beauty and progress that characterize human civilization endure with it.

References

Introduction: The Tailor's Art

1 M. A. Laugier, *Essai sur l'architecture* (Paris, 1753).
2 A. Loos, 'Praise for the Present', in *Adolf Loos: Why a Man Should be Well Dressed*, trans. M. E. Troy (Vienna, 2011), pp. 14–15.
3 E. Ostick, *Textiles for Tailors* (London, c. 1950).
4 N. Owen and A. Cannon Jones, 'A Comparative Study of the British and Italian Textile and Clothing Industries', *DTI Economics Paper*, II (2003), pp. 38–9.
5 Ibid., p. 39.
6 S. Vincent, *Dressing the Elite: Clothes in Early Modern England* (Oxford, 2003), pp. 104–7. C. Collier Frick, *Dressing Renaissance Florence: Families, Fortunes and Fine Clothing* (Baltimore, MD, 2002), pp. 228–30. See also U. Rublack, *Dressing Up: Cultural Identity in Renaissance Europe* (Oxford, 2010).
7 E. Currie, 'Diversity and Design in the Florentine Tailoring Trade, 1550–1620', in *The Material Renaissance*, ed. M. O'Malley and E. Welch (Manchester, 2007), p. 154.
8 Ibid., pp. 163–8.
9 D. Kuchta, *The Three-piece Suit and Modern Masculinity: England, 1550–1850* (Berkeley, CA, 2002), pp. 162–78.
10 J. C. Flügel, *The Psychology of Clothes* (London, 1930), p. 113.
11 Kuchta, *The Three-piece Suit*, pp. 17–50.
12 A. Hollander, *Sex and Suits: The Evolution of Modern Dress* (New York, 1995), pp. 63–110.

13 C. Breward, 'Manliness, Modernity and the Shaping of Male Clothing', in *Body Dressing*, ed. J. Entwistle and E. Wilson (Oxford, 2001), p. 166.

14 E. Giles, *History of the Art of Cutting in England* (London, 1887), p. 118.

15 Ibid., p. 124.

16 Quoted ibid., p. 133.

17 C. Compaing and L. Devere, *The Tailor's Guide* (London, 1855), pp. 18–19.

18 Giles, *History of the Art of Cutting*, p. 144.

19 Quoted ibid., p. 150.

20 Quoted ibid.

21 This catchphrase was used in a recurring 'menswear' sketch that appeared in the influential Charlie Higson/Paul Whitehouse BBC comedy *The Fast Show* between 1994 and 1997.

22 T. H. Holding, *The Tailor and Cutter*, 15 July 1880, p. 245.

23 J. B. Paoletti, 'Ridicule and Role Models as Factors in American Men's Fashion Change 1880–1910', *Costume*, XXXIX (1985), pp. 121–34.

24 Anon., 'The New Style of Tailoring', *The London Tailor*, 13 August 1898, p. 1.

25 Owen and Jones, 'A Comparative Study', p. 52.

26 Hollander, *Sex and Suits*, p. 3.

ONE: Well Suited

1 E. Carpenter, 'Simplification of Life' (London, 1886), quoted in B. Burman, 'Better and Brighter Clothes: The Men's Dress Reform Party, 1929–1940', *Journal of Design History*, VIII/4 (1995), p. 275.

2 D. Kuchta, *The Three-piece Suit and Modern Masculinity: England, 1550–1850* (Berkeley, CA, 2002), p. 80.

3 Quoted ibid., p. 82.

4 T. S. Abler, *Hinterland Warriors and Military Dress: European Empires and Exotic Uniforms* (Oxford, 1999), pp. 11–13.

5 D. Roche, *The Culture of Clothing: Dress and Fashion in the Ancien Regime* (Cambridge, 1994), p. 237.

6 Ibid., p. 229.

7 Ibid., p. 231.

8 J. Styles, *The Dress of the People: Everyday Fashion in Eighteenth-century England* (New Haven, CT, 2012), pp. 49–51.

9 Ibid., pp. 202–5.

10 Quoted ibid., p. 206.

11 J. Harvey, *Men in Black* (London, 1995), p. 158.

12 Ibid., p. 193.

13 Quoted in C. Breward, 'On the Bank's Threshold: Administrative Revolutions and the Fashioning of Masculine Identities', *Parallax*, V (1997), p. 112.

14 Ibid., p. 111.

15 H. Dennis Bradley, *Vogue: A Clothing Catalogue for Pope and Bradley* (London, 1912), pp. 12–13.

16 M. Zakim, *Ready-made Democracy: A History of Men's Dress in the American Republic, 1760–1860* (Chicago, IL, 2003), p. 126.

17 S. Pearson, *Week Day Living: A Book for Young Men and Women* (London, 1882), p. 139.

18 J. Greenwood, *Odd People in Odd Places; or, The Great Residuum* (London, 1883), pp. 82–3.

19 J. Tynan, 'Military Dress and Men's Outdoor Leisurewear: Burberry's Trench Coat in First World War Britain', *Journal of Design History*, XXIV/2 (2011), p. 140.

20 Quoted ibid., p. 141.

21 Ibid., p. 154.

22 F. Mort, *Cultures of Consumption: Masculinities and Social Space in Late Twentieth Century Britain* (London, 1996), p. 135.

23 Ibid., pp. 138–9.

24 H. Amies, *Just So Far* (London, 1954), p. 245.

25 P. A. Cunningham, 'Dressing for Success: The Re-suiting of Corporate America in the 1970s', in *Twentieth-century*

American Fashion, ed. L. Welters and P. A. Cunningham (Oxford, 2005), pp. 191–208.

26 G. Bruce Boyer, *Elegance: A Guide to Quality in Menswear* (New York, 1985), pp. 55–6.

27 P. York, *Style Wars* (London, 1980), p. 61.

28 Ibid., p. 65.

29 Quoted in D. Kynaston, *The City of London*, vol. IV: *A Club No More, 1945–2000* (London, 2001), p. 716.

30 Quoted in *Financial Times Weekend*, 13 March 1993, p. xix.

31 *The Times*, 11 September 2000, p. 17.

32 C. Evans, 'Fashion Stranger than Fiction: Shelley Fox', in *The Englishness of English Dress*, ed. C. Breward, B. Conekin and C. Cox (Oxford, 2002), pp. 206–7. See also T. Carver, *The Postmodern Marx* (Manchester, 1998); and P. Stallybrass, 'Marx's Coat', in *Border Fetishisms: Material Objects in Unstable Spaces*, ed. P. Spyer (New York, 1998).

33 Stallybrass, 'Marx's Coat', p. 196, quoted in C. Evans, *Fashion at the Edge: Spectacle, Modernity and Deathliness* (New Haven, CT, and London, 2003), p. 257.

TWO: Suiting Nations

1 H. Amies, *The Englishman's Suit* (London, 1994), pp. 104–10.

2 Samuel Pepys, diary entry 1 July 1661, available at www.pepysdiary.com (accessed 27 August 2013).

3 Samuel Pepys, diary entry 30 March 1666, available at www.pepysdiary.com (accessed 27 August 2013).

4 A. Settle, *English Fashion* (London, 1948), p. 48.

5 P. York, 'Icons of Identity', *Country Life*, 1 February 1996, pp. 28–31.

6 S. Hall, 'Culture, Community, Nation', in *Representing the Nation: A Reader*, ed. D. Boswell and J. Evans (London, 1999), p. 42.

7 K. Hearn, ed., *Van Dyck and Britain* (London, 2009), p. 98.

8 A. Hart and S. North, *Seventeenth- and Eighteenth-century Fashion in Detail* (London, 2009), p. 130.

9 D. Maglio, 'Luxuriant Crowns: Victorian Men's Smoking Caps, 1850–1890', *Dress: The Journal of the Costume Society of America*, XXVII (2000), pp. 9–17.

10 E. Armfeldt, 'Oriental London', in *Living London*, ed. G. Sims, vol. I (London, 1906), pp. 81–2.

11 J. MacKenzie, ed., *Imperialism and Popular Culture* (Manchester, 1986).

12 H. Callaway, 'Dressing for Dinner in the Bush: Rituals of Self-definition and British Imperial Authority', in *Dress and Gender: Making and Meaning*, ed. R. Barnes and J. B. Eicher (Oxford, 1992), p. 241.

13 V. Wilson, 'Dressing for Leadership in China', in *Material Strategies: Dress and Gender in Historical Perspective*, ed. B. Burman and C. Turbin (Oxford, 2003), pp. 239–42.

14 Ibid., p. 244.

15 Ibid., p. 249.

16 Ibid., p. 251.

17 R. Ross, *Clothing: A Global History* (Cambridge, 2008), p. 159.

18 J. J. Wu, *Chinese Fashion: From Mao to Now* (Oxford, 2009), p. 3.

19 Wilson, 'Dressing for Leadership', p. 250.

20 T. Slade, *Japanese Fashion: A Cultural History* (Oxford, 2009), p. 81.

21 Ibid., pp. 92–4.

22 L. Dalby, *Kimono: Fashioning Culture* (London, 2001), p. 58.

23 V. Steele, *Japan Fashion Now* (New Haven, 2010), p. 10.

24 Ibid., pp. 13–14.

25 Ross, *Clothing*, p. 111.

26 D. Tamagni, *Gentlemen of Bacongo* (London, 2007).

THREE: Sharp Suits

1 G. Walden, trans., 'Jules Barbey d'Aurevilly, "On Dandyism and George Brummell"', in *Who's a Dandy?* (London, 2002), p. 79.

2 M. Carter, *Fashion Classics: From Carlyle to Barthes*
   (Oxford, 2003), p. 11.

3 H. de Balzac, *Treatise on Elegant Living* (Cambridge, MA,
   2010), pp. 25, 58 and 70.

4 C. Baudelaire, 'The Dandy', from *The Painter of Modern
   Life*, in *The Rise of Fashion: A Reader*, ed. D. Purdy
   (Minneapolis, MN, 2004), pp. 194–5.

5 See E. Moers, *The Dandy* (New York, 1960); R. Garelick,
   *Rising Star: Dandyism, Gender and Performance in the
   Fin de Siecle* (Princeton, NJ, 1998); and S. Fillin-Yeh, ed.,
   Dandies: Fashion and Finesse in Art and Culture (New
   York, 2001).

6 See M. Duberman, M. Vicinus and G. Chauncey, eds,
   Hidden from History: Reclaiming the Gay and Lesbian Past
   (London, 1989); R. Norton, *Mother Clapp's Molly House:
   The Gay Subculture in England, 1700–1830* (London, 1992);
   and R. Aldrich, *Gay Life and Culture: A World History*
   (London, 2006).

7 R. Davenport-Hines, *Sex, Death and Punishment: Attitudes
   to Sex and Sexuality in Britain Since the Renaissance*
   (London, 1990), p. 86; and R. Trumbach, 'The Birth of the
   Queen: Sodomy and the Emergence of Gender Equality in
   Modern Culture, 1660–1750', in *Hidden from History*, ed.
   Duberman, Vicinus and Chauncey, p. 135.

8 Quoted in Trumbach, 'The Birth of the Queen', p. 133.

9 T. Smollett, *The Adventures of Roderick Random*
   (London, 1895), p. 239.

10 M. Ogborn, *Spaces of Modernity: London's Geographies,
   1680–1780* (New York, 1998), p. 134. See also P. McNeil,
   'Macaroni Masculinities', *Fashion Theory*, IV/4
   (November 2000), pp. 373–403.

11 Quoted in Ogborn, *Spaces of Modernity*, pp. 137–8.

12 H. Cole, *Beau Brummell* (Newton Abbot, 1978); I. Kelly,
   Beau Brummell: The Ultimate Dandy (London, 2005).

13 W. Jesse, *The Life of George Beau Brummell Esq.*
   (London, 1886), p. 63.

14 Ibid., pp. 62–3.

15 R. Gronow, *Reminiscences of Captain Gronow* (London, 1862), p. 62.

16 R. Ellmann, *Oscar Wilde* (London, 1987); J. Sloan, *Oscar Wilde* (Oxford, 2003).

17 B. Burman, 'Better and Brighter Clothes: The Men's Dress Reform Party, 1929–1940', *Journal of Design History*, VIII/4 (1995), pp. 275–90.

18 E. Cohen, *Talk on the Wilde Side* (London, 1993); A. Sinfield, *The Wilde Century* (London, 1994).

19 M. Boscagli, *Eye on the Flesh: Fashions of Masculinity in the Early Twentieth Century* (Oxford, 1996), pp. 33–4.

20 L. Ugolini, *Men and Menswear: Sartorial Consumption in Britai, 1880–1939* (Aldershot, 2007), pp. 253–5.

21 Garelick, *Rising Star*.

22 S. Cosgrove, 'The Zoot Suit and Style Warfare', *History Workshop Journal*, XVIII (1984), pp. 77–91; K. Peiss, *Zoot Suit: The Enigmatic Career of an Extreme Style* (Philadelphia, PA, 2011).

23 H. Alford, 'The Zoot Suit: Its History and Influence', in *The Men's Fashion Reader*, ed. P. McNeil and V. Karaminas (Oxford, 2009), p. 354.

24 R. H. Turner and S. J. Surace, 'Zoot-suiters and Mexicans: Symbols in Crowd Behavior', in *The Subcultures Reader*, ed. K. Gelder and S. Thornton (London, 1997), p. 382.

25 Quoted in C. Tulloch, 'My Man, Let Me Pull your Coat to Something: Malcolm X', in *Fashion Cultures: Theories, Explanations and Analysis*, ed. S. Bruzzi and P. Church Gibson (London, 2000), p. 304.

26 C. Breward, *Fashioning London: Clothing and the Modern Metropolis* (Oxford, 2004), p. 126.

27 H. D. Willcock, *Mass Observation Report on Juvenile Delinquency* (London, 1949), p. 41.

28 D. Bartlett, 'Socialist Dandies International: East Europe, 1946–59', *Fashion Theory*, XVII/3 (June 2013), p. 250.

29 P. Colaiacomo, *Factious Elegance: Pasolini and Male Fashion* (Venice, 2007).

30 F. Chenoune, *A History of Men's Fashion* (Paris, 1993).

31 G. Celant, 'Towards the Mass Dandy', in *Giorgio Armani* (New York, 2003), p. xviii.

32 Colaiacomo, *Factious Elegance*, p. 56.

33 P. Pasolini, 'The Divine Mimesis, Canto II, 1963. 24', quoted ibid., p. 58.

34 V. Steele, 'The Italian Look', in *Volare: The Icon of Italy in Global Pop Culture*, ed. Giannino Malossi (New York, 1999), p. 91.

35 Colaiacomo, *Factious Elegance*, pp. 105–7.

36 Celant, 'Towards the Mass Dandy', p. xvii.

37 Ibid., p. xv.

38 C. Breward, 'Camp and the International Language of 1970s Fashion', in *Walter Albini and his Times: All Power to the Imagination*, ed. M. L. Frisa and S. Tonchi (Venice, 2010), p. 16.

39 S. Segre Reinach, 'Milan: The City of Prêt à Porter in a World of Fast Fashion', in *Fashion's World Cities*, ed. C. Breward and D. Gilbert (Oxford, 2006), p. 123–5.

40 R. Buckley and S. Gundle, 'Flash Trash: Gianni Versace and the Theory and Practice of Glamour', in *Fashion Cultures*, pp. 331–48.

41 K. Nelson, 'Playboy', in *Gucci: The Making Of* (New York, 2011), pp. 208 and 280.

42 J. Wilkes, 'Tom Ford', in *Gucci*, p. 54.

43 L. Taylor, 'Wool Cloth and Gender: The Use of Woollen Cloth in Women's Dress in Britain, 1865–1885', in *Defining Dress: Dress as Object, Meaning and Identity*, ed. A. de la Haye and E. Wilson (Manchester, 1999), p. 33.

44 P. A. Cunningham, *Reforming Women's Fashion, 1850–1920* (Kent, OH, 2003).

45 M. Garber, *Vested Interests: Cross-dressing and Cultural Anxiety* (London, 1992); V. and B. Bulloch, *Cross Dressing, Sex and Gender* (Philadelphia, PA, 1993).

46 K. Rolley, 'Love, Desire and the Pursuit of the Whole: Dress and the Lesbian Couple', in *Chic Thrills: A Fashion Reader*, ed. J. Ash and E. Wilson (London, 1992), p. 34.

47 V. de Frece, *Recollections of Vesta Tilley* (London, 1934), p. 125.
48 E. Showalter, *Sexual Anarchy: Gender and Culture at the Fin-de-siècle* (London, 1992).
49 S. Gundle, *Glamour: A History* (Oxford, 2008), p. 325.

FOUR: Seeing the Suit

1 H. C. Andersen, *The Emperor's New Clothes* (London, 1995), p. 1.
2 J. Wullschlager, *Hans Christian Andersen: The Life of a Storyteller* (London, 2001), p. 170.
3 Andersen, *The Emperor's New Clothes*, p. 7.
4 A. Loos, 'The Principle of Dressing', in M. Wigley, *White Walls, Designer Dresses: The Fashion of Modern Architecture* (Cambridge, MA, 2001), p. 13.
5 Wigley, *White Walls*, p. 12.
6 Le Corbusier, 'Towards a New Architecture', in Wigley, *White Walls*, p. 16.
7 Le Corbusier, *The Decorative Art of Today*, trans. James Dunnett (London, 1987), p. xxiii.
8 Ibid., p. 7.
9 Ibid., p. 8.
10 Ibid., p. 87.
11 Wigley, *White Walls*, pp. 90–91.
12 B. Colomina, 'The Split Wall: Domestic Voyeurism', in *Sexuality and Space*, ed. B. Colomina (New York, 1992), pp. 73–130.
13 R. Stern, *Against Fashion: Clothing as Art, 1850–1930* (Cambridge, MA, 2004), pp. 31–2.
14 Quoted ibid., pp. 157–8.
15 Quoted ibid., p. 167.
16 F. Chenoune, *A History of Men's Fashion* (Paris, 1993), p. 170.
17 H. Brevik-Zender, 'Writing Fashion from Balzac to Mallarme', in *Impressionism, Fashion and Modernity*, ed. G. Groom (New Haven, CT, 2012), p. 54.

18 Quoted in P. Thiébaut, 'An Ideal of Virile Urbanity', in
    Impressionism, Fashion and Modernity, ed. Groom, p. 142.

19 R. Violette and H. U. Obrist, eds, *The Words of Gilbert
    and George* (London, 1997), pp. 260–61.

20 M. L. Miller, *Slaves to Fashion: Black Dandyism and the
    Styling of Black Diasporic Identity* (Durham, NC, and
    London, 2009), p. 221.

21 Quoted ibid., p. 219.

22 G. Adamson and J. Pavitt, *Postmodernism: Style and
    Subversion, 1970–1990* (London, 2011), p. 94.

23 U. Lehmann, 'Language of the PurSuit: Cary Grant's
    Clothes in Alfred Hitchcock's *North by Northwest*',
    Fashion Theory, IV/4 (December 2000), pp. 467–85.

24 J. Faiers, *Dressing Dangerously: Dysfunctional Fashion
    in Film* (New Haven, CT, and London, 2013), p. 227.

25 Ibid., pp. 189–90.

26 C. McDowell, *Forties Fashion and the New Look*
    (London, 1997); see also C. Breward, *Fashion*
    (Oxford, 2003), pp. 174–7.

27 A. Spicer, 'Sean Connery: Loosening his Bonds', in *British
    Stars and Stardom: From Alma Taylor to Sean Connery*,
    ed. B. Babington (Manchester, 2001), pp. 220–21.

28 C. Woodhead, ed., *Dressed to Kill: James Bond, The Suited
    Hero* (Paris and New York, 1996).

29 See www.thesuitsofjamesbond.com, accessed January 2015.

30 Susannah Frankel, *AnOther Man* (Autumn/Winter 2006),
    p. 143.

31 See C. Evans, *Fashion at the Edge: Spectacle, Modernity
    and Deathliness* (New Haven, CT, and London, 2003),
    for the most informed discussion on this turn in
    fashion's history.

Epilogue: Future Suits

1 A. O'Hagan, 'Short Cuts', *London Review of Books*,
   3 July 2014, p. 23.

2 S. Nixon, *Hard Looks: Masculinities, Spectatorship and Contemporary Consumption* (London, 1996); T. Edwards, *Men in the Mirror: Men's Fashion, Masculinity and Consumer Society* (London, 1997).

3 J. Teiunisson, 'Why is Menswear in Fashion?', in *The New Man*, ed. J. Brand et al. (Arnhem, 2010), pp. 7–27.

4 Quoted in H. Davies, *Modern Menswear* (London, 2008), p. 11.

5 R. Bennett-England, *Dress Optional: A Revolution in Menswear* (London, 1967).

6 B. Quinn, *Techno Fashion* (Oxford, 2002).

Select Bibliography

Abler, T. S., *Hinterland Warriors and Military Dress: European Empires and Exotic Uniforms* (Oxford, 1999)

Adamson, G., and J. Pavitt, *Postmodernism: Style and Subversion, 1970–1990* (London, 2011)

Aldrich, R., *Gay Life and Culture: A World History* (London, 2006)

Alford, H., 'The Zoot Suit: Its History and Influence', in *The Men's Fashion Reader*, ed. P. McNeil and V. Karaminas (Oxford, 2009)

Amies, H., *Just So Far* (London, 1954)

—, *The Englishman's Suit* (London, 1994)

Andersen, H. C., *The Emperor's New Clothes* (London, 1995)

Armfeldt, E., 'Oriental London', in *Living London*, ed. G. Sims, vol. I (London, 1906)

Balzac, H. de, *Treatise on Elegant Living* (Cambridge, MA, 2010)

Bartlett, D., 'Socialist Dandies International: East Europe, 1946–59', *Fashion Theory*, XVII/3 (June 2013), pp. 249–89

Baudelaire, C., 'The Dandy', from *The Painter of Modern Life*, in *The Rise of Fashion: A Reader*, ed. D. Purdy (Minneapolis, MN, 2004)

Boscagli, M., *Eye on the Flesh: Fashions of Masculinity in the Early Twentieth Century* (Oxford, 1996)

Boyer, G. Bruce, *Elegance: A Guide to Quality in Menswear* (New York, 1985)

Bradley, H. Dennis, *Vogue: A Clothing Catalogue for Pope and Bradley* (London, 1912)

Brevik-Zender, H., 'Writing Fashion from Balzac to Mallarme', in *Impressionism, Fashion and Modernity*, ed. G. Groom (New Haven, CT, 2012)

Breward, C., 'On the Bank's Threshold: Administrative Revolutions and the Fashioning of Masculine Identities', *Parallax*, V (1997), pp. 109–23

—, *The Hidden Consumer: Masculinities, Fashion and City Life, 1860–1914* (Manchester, 1999)

—, 'Manliness, Modernity and the Shaping of Male Clothing', in *Body Dressing*, ed. J. Entwistle and E. Wilson (Oxford, 2001)

—, *Fashion* (Oxford, 2003)

—, *Fashioning London: Clothing and the Modern Metropolis* (Oxford, 2004)

—, 'Camp and the International Language of 1970s Fashion', in *Walter Albini and his Times: All Power to the Imagination*, ed. M. L. Frisa and S. Tonchi (Venice, 2010)

Buckley, R., and S. Gundle, 'Flash Trash: Gianni Versace and the Theory and Practice of Glamour', in *Fashion Cultures*, ed. S. Bruzzi and P. Church Gibson (London, 2000)

Bulloch, V. and B., *Cross Dressing, Sex and Gender* (Philadelphia, PA, 1993)

Burman, B., 'Better and Brighter Clothes: The Men's Dress Reform Party, 1929–1940', *Journal of Design History*, VIII/4 (1995), pp. 275–90

Callaway, H., 'Dressing for Dinner in the Bush: Rituals of Self-definition and British Imperial Authority', in *Dress and Gender: Making and Meaning*, ed. R. Barnes and J. B. Eicher (Oxford, 1992)

Carter, M., *Fashion Classics: From Carlyle to Barthes* (Oxford, 2003)

Carver, T., *The Postmodern Marx* (Manchester, 1998)

Celant, G., 'Towards the Mass Dandy', in *Giorgio Armani* (New York, 2003)

Chenoune, F., *A History of Men's Fashion* (Paris, 1993)

Cohen, E., *Talk on the Wilde Side* (London, 1993)

Colaiacomo, P., *Factious Elegance: Pasolini and Male Fashion* (Venice, 2007)

Cole, H., *Beau Brummell* (Newton Abbot, 1978)

Collier Frick, C., *Dressing Renaissance Florence: Families, Fortunes and Fine Clothing* (Baltimore, MD, 2002)

Colomina, B., ed., *Sexuality and Space* (New York, 1992)

Compaing, C., and L. Devere, *The Tailor's Guide* (London, 1855)

Cosgrove, S., 'The Zoot Suit and Style Warfare', *History Workshop Journal*, XVIII (1984), pp. 77–91

Cunningham, P. A., *Reforming Women's Fashion, 1850–1920* (Kent, OH, 2003)

—, 'Dressing for Success: The Re-suiting of Corporate America in the 1970s', in *Twentieth-century American Fashion*, ed. L. Welters and P. A. Cunningham (Oxford, 2005)

Currie, E., 'Diversity and Design in the Florentine Tailoring Trade, 1550–1620', in *The Material Renaissance*, ed. M. O'Malley and E. Welch (Manchester, 2007)

Dalby, L., *Kimono: Fashioning Culture* (London, 2001)

Davenport-Hines, R., *Sex, Death and Punishment: Attitudes to Sex and Sexuality in Britain Since the Renaissance* (London, 1990)

Duberman, M., M. Vicinus and G. Chauncey, eds, *Hidden from History: Reclaiming the Gay and Lesbian Past* (London, 1989)

Ellmann, R., *Oscar Wilde* (London, 1987)

Evans, C., 'Fashion Stranger than Fiction: Shelley Fox', in *The Englishness of English Dress*, ed. C. Breward, B. Conekin and C. Cox (Oxford, 2002)

—, *Fashion at the Edge: Spectacle, Modernity and Deathliness* (New Haven, CT, and London, 2003)

Faiers, J., *Dressing Dangerously: Dysfunctional Fashion in Film* (New Haven, CT, and London, 2013)

Fillin-Yeh, S., ed., *Dandies: Fashion and Finesse in Art and Culture* (New York, 2001)

Flügel, J. C., *The Psychology of Clothes* (London, 1930)

Frece, V. de, *Recollections of Vesta Tilley* (London, 1934)

Garber, M., *Vested Interests: Cross-dressing and Cultural Anxiety* (London, 1992)

Garelick, R. K., *Rising Star: Dandyism, Gender and Performance in the Fin de Siècle* (Princeton, NJ, 1998)

Giles, E., *History of the Art of Cutting in England* (London, 1887)

Greenwood, J., *Odd People in Odd Places; or, The Great Residuum* (London, 1883)

Gronow, R., *Reminiscences of Captain Gronow* (London, 1862)

Gundle, S., *Glamour: A History* (Oxford, 2008)

Hall, S., 'Culture, Community, Nation', in *Representing the Nation: A Reader*, ed. D. Boswell and J. Evans (London, 1999)

Hart, A., and S. North, *Seventeenth- and Eighteenth-century Fashion in Detail* (London, 2009)

Harvey, J., *Men in Black* (London, 1995)

Hearn, K., ed., *Van Dyck and Britain* (London, 2009)

Hollander, A., *Sex and Suits: The Evolution of Modern Dress* (New York, 1995)

Jesse, W., *The Life of George Beau Brummell Esq.* (London, 1886)

Kelly, I., *Beau Brummell: The Ultimate Dandy* (London, 2005)

Kuchta, D., *The Three Piece Suit and Modern Masculinity: England, 1550–1850* (Berkeley, CA, 2002)

Kynaston, D., *The City of London*, vol. IV: *A Club No More, 1945–2000* (London, 2001)

Laugier, M. A., *Essai sur l'architecture* (Paris, 1753)

Le Corbusier, *The Decorative Art of Today*, trans. James Dunnett (London, 1987)

Lehmann, U., 'Language of the PurSuit: Cary Grant's Clothes in Alfred Hitchcock's *North by Northwest*', *Fashion Theory*, IV/4 (December 2000), pp. 467–85

Loos, A., 'Praise for the Present', in *Adolf Loos: Why a Man Should be Well Dressed*, trans. M. E. Troy (Vienna, 2011)

McDowell, C., *Forties Fashion and the New Look* (London, 1997)

MacKenzie, J., ed., *Imperialism and Popular Culture* (Manchester, 1986)

McNeil, P., 'Macaroni Masculinities', *Fashion Theory*, IV/4 (November 2000), pp. 373–403

—, and V. Karaminas, eds, *The Men's Fashion Reader* (Oxford, 2009)

Maglio, D., 'Luxuriant Crowns: Victorian Men's Smoking Caps, 1850–1890', *Dress: The Journal of the Costume Society of America*, XXVII (2000), pp. 9–17

Miller, M. L., *Slaves to Fashion: Black Dandyism and the Styling of Black Diasporic Identity* (Durham, NC, and London, 2009)

Moers, E., *The Dandy* (New York, 1960)

Mort, F., *Cultures of Consumption: Masculinities and Social Space in Late Twentieth Century Britain* (London, 1996)

Nelson, K., 'Playboy', in *Gucci: The Making Of* (New York, 2011)

Norton, R., *Mother Clapp's Molly House: The Gay Subculture in England, 1700–1830* (London, 1992)

Ogborn, M., *Spaces of Modernity: London's Geographies, 1680–1780* (New York, 1998)

Ostick, E., *Textiles for Tailors* (London, c. 1950)

Owen, N., and A. Cannon Jones, 'A Comparative Study of the British and Italian Textile and Clothing Industries', *DTI Economics Paper*, II (2003)

Paoletti, J. B., 'Ridicule and Role Models as Factors in American Men's Fashion Change, 1880–1910', *Costume*, XXXIX (1985), pp. 121–34

Pearson, S., *Week Day Living: A Book for Young Men and Women* (London, 1882)

Peiss, K., *Zoot Suit: The Enigmatic Career of an Extreme Style* (Philadelphia, PA, 2011)

Roche, D., *The Culture of Clothing: Dress and Fashion in the Ancien Regime* (Cambridge, 1994)

Rolley, K., 'Love, Desire and the Pursuit of the Whole: Dress and the Lesbian Couple', in *Chic Thrills: A Fashion Reader*, ed. J. Ash and E. Wilson (London, 1992)

Ross, R., *Clothing: A Global History* (Cambridge, 2008)

Rublack, U., *Dressing Up: Cultural Identity in Renaissance Europe* (Oxford, 2010)

Segre Reinach, S., 'Milan: The City of Prêt à Porter in a World of Fast Fashion', in *Fashion's World Cities*, ed. C. Breward and D. Gilbert (Oxford, 2006)

Settle, A., *English Fashion* (London, 1948)

Showalter, E., *Sexual Anarchy: Gender and Culture at the Fin-de-siècle* (London, 1992)

Sinfield, A., *The Wilde Century* (London, 1994)

Slade, T., *Japanese Fashion: A Cultural History* (Oxford, 2009)

Sloan, J., *Oscar Wilde* (Oxford, 2003)

Smollett, T., *The Adventures of Roderick Random* (London, 1895)

Spicer, A., 'Sean Connery: Loosening his Bonds', in *British Stars and Stardom: From Alma Taylor to Sean Connery*, ed. B. Babington (Manchester, 2001)

Stallybrass, P., 'Marx's Coat', in *Border Fetishisms: Material Objects in Unstable Spaces*, ed. P. Spyer (New York, 1998)

Steele, V., 'The Italian Look', in *Volare: The Icon of Italy in Global Pop Culture*, ed. Giannino Malossi (New York, 1999)

—, *Japan Fashion Now* (New Haven, CT, 2010)

Stern, R., *Against Fashion: Clothing as Art, 1850–1930* (Cambridge, MA, 2004)

Styles, J., *The Dress of the People: Everyday Fashion in Eighteenth-century England* (New Haven, CT, 2012)

Tamagni, D., *Gentlemen of Bacongo* (London, 2007)

Taylor, L., 'Wool Cloth and Gender: The Use of Woollen Cloth in Women's Dress in Britain, 1865–1885', in *Defining Dress: Dress as Object, Meaning and Identity*, ed. A. de la Haye and E. Wilson (Manchester, 1999)

Thiébaut, P., 'An Ideal of Virile Urbanity', in *Impressionism, Fashion and Modernity*, ed. G. Groom (New Haven, CT, 2012)

Trumbach, R., 'The Birth of the Queen: Sodomy and the Emergence of Gender Equality in Modern Culture 1660–1750', in *Hidden from History: Reclaiming the Gay and Lesbian Past*, ed. M. Duberman, M. Vicinus and G. Chauncey (London, 1989)

Tulloch, C., 'My Man, Let Me Pull your Coat to Something: Malcolm X', in *Fashion Cultures: Theories, Explanations and Analysis*, ed. S. Bruzzi and P. Church Gibson (London, 2000)

Turner, R. H., and S. J. Surace, 'Zoot-suiters and Mexicans: Symbols in Crowd Behavior', in *The Subcultures Reader*, ed. K. Gelder and S. Thornton (London, 1997)

Tynan, J., 'Military Dress and Men's Outdoor Leisurewear: Burberry's Trench Coat in First World War Britain', *Journal of Design History*, xxiv/2 (2011), pp. 139–56

Ugolini, L., *Men and Menswear: Sartorial Consumption in Britain, 1880–1939* (Aldershot, 2007)

Vincent, S., *Dressing the Elite: Clothes in Early Modern England* (Oxford, 2003)

Violette, R., and H. Ulrich Obrist, eds, *The Words of Gilbert and George* (London, 1997)

Walden, G., trans., 'Jules Barbey d'Aurevilly, "On Dandyism and George Brummell"', in *Who's a Dandy?* (London, 2002)

Wigley, M., *White Walls, Designer Dresses: The Fashion of Modern Architecture* (Cambridge, MA, 2001)

Willcock, H. D., *Mass Observation Report on Juvenile Delinquency* (London, 1949)

Wilson, V., 'Dressing for Leadership in China', in *Material Strategies: Dress and Gender in Historical Perspective*, ed. B. Burman and C. Turbin (Oxford, 2003)

Woodhead, C., ed., *Dressed to Kill: James Bond, The Suited Hero* (Paris and New York, 1996)

Wu, J. J., *Chinese Fashion: From Mao to Now* (Oxford, 2009)

Wullschlager, J., *Hans Christian Andersen: The Life of a Storyteller* (London, 2001)

York, P., *Style Wars* (London, 1980)

Zakim, M., *Ready-made Democracy: A History of Men's Dress in the American Republic, 1760–1860* (Chicago, IL, 2003)

Acknowledgements

The completion of this book has been made possible by the patience and professional advice of editorial director Vivian Constantino-poulos, the administrative assistance of Anne Mackenna, the picture research skills of Elisabeth Gernerd, the financial support of the Research Committee of Edinburgh College of Art at the University of Edinburgh and the Carnegie Trust for the Universities of Scotland, the valuable intellectual and practical contributions of former and present colleagues at the Victoria & Albert Museum and the University of Edinburgh, and all those who have suggested avenues of research at conferences and seminars, the generosity of those owners of pictures and archives who have allowed their reproduction here, and the domestic forbearance of my partner, James Brook.

Photo Acknowledgements

Image courtesy of The Advertising Archives: p. 69; Anderson & Sheppard: pp. 11, 14, 23; © The British Library Board: pp. 124, 166; Corbis: pp. 103 (© Jason Lee/Reuters), 111 (© Héctor Mediaville/PT/Splash/Splash News); Marisa Curti Archive/Walter Albini: p. 150; Getty Images: pp. 66 (Reg Innell/Toronto Star via Getty Images), 171 (Keystone-France/Gamma-Keystone via Getty Images); Houghton Library, Harvard University: p. 180 (IC9.M3387.B922f); Harvard Art Museums/Arthur M. Sackler Museum, Bequest of William S. Lieberman, 2007.214.102.2, Imaging Department © President and Fellows of Harvard College: p. 106; © Imperial War Museums: pp. 58 (Q 90901), 59 (Art.IWM PST 5072), 60 (Art.IWM PST 12902); courtesy of Richard James: p. 204 (photo: Vivian Constantinopoulos); Library of Congress, Washington, DC: p. 51; Metropolitan Museum of Art, New York, www.metmuseum.org: pp. 42 (Bequest of William K. Vanderbilt, 1920), 50 (Gift of Miss Jeanne Devereaux, 1951), 82 (Amelia B. Lazarus Fund, 1923), 122 (Purchase, Friends of the Costume Institute Gifts), 185 (The Walter H. and Leonore Annenberg Collection, Bequest of Walter H. Annenberg, 2002); Museum of Applied Arts and Sciences, Sydney. Photo: Sue Strafford: pp. 97, 101; © 2015 Museum Associates/LACMA. Licensed by Art Resource, NY: p. 37; photograph © 2016 Museum of Fine Arts, Boston: p. 18 (The Elizabeth Day McCormick Collection); National Australian Archives, Vienna: p. 9; © The Helmut Newton Estate/Maconochie Photography: p. 164; The New York Public Library, Astor, Lenox and Tilden Foundations: pp. 33 (Picture Collection), 62 (Art &

Architecture Collection, Miriam and Ira D. Wallach Division of Art, Prints and Photographs), 63 (Science, Industry & Business Library), 178 (Picture Collection); Photofest: pp. 75 (© Paramount Pictures), 93 (RKO), 95, 99, 135 (© 20th Century Fox), 140 (Brandon Films), 147, 192 (Cinecom), 193 (MGM), 195 (Ealing Studios/J.Arthur Rank.Org), 196, 198 (© MGM/ Columbia Pictures/Francois Duhamel); REX Shutterstock: pp. 34 (Roger-Viollet), 35, 70 (Paul Flevez/ANL), 78 (ANL), 109 (Sipa), 114 (David Crump/ANL), 133 (ANL), 143 (Sipa Press), 144–5 (ANL), 153 (Olycom SPA), 156 (Ken Towner), 157 (Nils Jorgensen), 186, 200 (Olycom SPA), 206, 207 (Chris Ratcliffe), 208 (David Hartley), 209, 211 (SPG); Rijksmuseum, Amsterdam: p. 19; Science & Society Picture Library: pp. 55 (PastPix), 64 (Walter Numberg Archive), 138 (Manchester Daily Express); courtesy of the artist (Iké Udé) and Leila Heller Gallery, New York: p. 189; The University of Edinburgh Fine Art Collection, Edinburgh: p. 27; © Victoria & Albert Museum, London: pp. 6, 16, 48, 83, 90, 91, 120, 163; courtesy of the Lewis Walpole Library, Yale University: pp. 117, 121, 128, 177; © Woolmark Archive (Australian Wool Innovation Ltd) and the London College of Fashion: pp. 30–31, 79, 108, 136, 159.

Index

Page numbers in italic refer to illustrations